# CHANGING MEN, TRANSFORMING CULTURE

# THE YALE CULTURAL SOCIOLOGY SERIES

Jeffrey C. Alexander and Ron Eyerman, Series Editors

PUBLISHED

*Triumph and Trauma,* by Bernhard Giesen (2004)

*Myth, Meaning, and Performance: Toward a New Cultural Sociology of the Arts,* edited by Ron Eyerman and Lisa McCormick (2006)

*American Society: A Theory of Societal Community,* by Talcott Parsons, edited and introduced by Giuseppe Sciortino (2007)

*The Easternization of the West,* by Colin Campbell (2007)

*Culture, Society, and Democracy: The Interpretive Approach,* edited by Isaac Reed and Jeffrey C. Alexander (2007)

*Changing Men, Transforming Culture: Inside the Men's Movement,* by Eric Magnuson (2007)

*Do We Need Religion? On the Experience of Self-Transcendence,* by Hans Joas (2007)

*A Contemporary Introduction to Sociology: Culture and Society in Transition,* by Jeffrey C. Alexander and Kenneth Thompson (2008)

FORTHCOMING

*Making Los Angeles: How People Create Place Out of Ordinary Urban Space,* by Christopher D. Campbell

*Jihadi Terrorism in the Modern World,* by Farhad Khosrokhavar

*Setting the Stage for a "New" South Africa: A Cultural Approach to the Truth and Reconciliation Commission,* by Tanya Goodman

*Meaning and Method: The Cultural Approach to Sociology,* edited by Isaac Reed and Jeffrey C. Alexander

# CHANGING MEN, TRANSFORMING CULTURE

## INSIDE THE MEN'S MOVEMENT

*Eric Magnuson*

*Paradigm Publishers*
Boulder • London

Published in the United States by Paradigm Publishers, 3360 Mitchell Lane Suite E, Boulder, CO 80301 USA.

Paradigm Publishers is the trade name of Birkenkamp & Company, LLC, Dean Birkenkamp, President and Publisher.

Library of Congress Cataloging-in-Publication Data

Magnuson, Eric Paul, 1969–
  Changing men, transforming culture : inside the men's movement / Eric Magnuson.
    p. cm. — (Yale cultural sociology series)
  Includes bibliographical references and index.
  978-1-59451-394-7 (hc)
  978-1-59451-395-4 (pbk)
1. Men's movement—United States. 2. Masculinity—United States. I. Title.
HQ1090.3.M233 2007
305.310973—dc22

                                                      2006035796


Printed and bound in the United States of America on acid-free paper that meets the standards of the American National Standard for Permanence of Paper for Printed Library Materials.

Designed and Typeset by Straight Creek Bookmakers.

11  10  09  08     2  3  4  5

To my mother, Sharon Magnuson,
whose courage and ceaseless efforts as a single mother
made this possible

# Contents

# Preface and Acknowledgments

The mythopoetic men's movement elicits a wide array of responses, ranging from surprise to knowing smirks, from fascination to disdain, and from enthusiastic support to bitter opposition. Images arise of men drumming in the woods, getting naked and jumping over campfires, and baring their souls as they cry amongst their fellow men. A number of years ago, I decided to look deeper into this strange and unique phenomenon. I sought to further develop contemporary cultural sociology and apply it to this curious social movement. This study is the result of that inquiry.

In the pages that follow, I examine the social construction of cultural discourse in the mythopoetic men's movement. Using ethnographic methods, this study is based on research spanning eight years of participant observation within the movement. Examining the ideological dynamics of the movement, the work analyzes the construction and negotiation of cultural discourse concerning masculinity, gender, and other perceived dominant ideologies of U.S. society. Using the concept of hegemony in a fully cultural way, the analysis examines the ways in which, in face-to-face interaction, the men of the movement develop structured moral understandings of a hegemonic masculinity and a hegemonic culture and, simultaneously, a counterhegemonic masculinity and counterhegemonic culture.

Theoretically, the study draws upon and advances contemporary cultural work in sociology to understand the structured systems of meaning constructed by the members of this movement. Developing this approach further, the analysis uses ethnographic data to forward understandings more sensitive to the microlevel dynamics of interaction, individual agency, and contingency. Further, issues of power and hegemony are included in ways that deepen the theoretical perspective while at the same time maintaining the fully cultural nature of the approach.

The members of the mythopoetic men's movement explicitly see themselves as reacting to a dominant form of gender identity they view as having limited and damaged both men and women. Their personal and political project is the formulation of a counterhegemonic masculinity. Overall, this is an organized, sustained identity creation movement. It is a seed movement, crystallizing new ideas about masculinity and creating new possibilities for the culture at large.

The men of the mythopoetic men's movement are also actively involved in the construction of critical interpretations of what they see as a dominant culture that stresses the importance of the work ethic, professional success, and material achievement. These men actively create alternative perspectives on the material sphere that decrease those priorities and increase the priorities of emotional growth, fathering, being a good partner, and being fully involved in family life. Related to this, they increase the importance of love, creativity, and spiritual pursuits. It is a distinct cultural shift they propose, one that has some potentially radical implications.

The mythopoetic men's movement has often been misunderstood in certain ways in both popular and academic circles. Many know little of the movement beyond the media caricatures of wild men beating drums in the woods and crying around bonfires. As this book will show, this is a gross stereotype that is shown to be false upon close empirical analysis.

A more subtle misunderstanding appears in many academic writings on the topic. Almost all scholarly work in the area has been based solely on analysis of the writings of popular texts that have inspired the movement (such as books by Robert Bly, Sam Keen, Michael Meade, and James Hillman). These writings have been easy to criticize as they are largely "pop psychology" and ungrounded creative mythology. They have an essentialist element as they call on men to rediscover some kind of innate masculinity that is seen as ahistorical, transcending time and place. The problem is that academic analysis almost always stops at that point. As a result, any work in this vein is not actually an empirical study of the movement itself. It cannot be determined what is going on within the movement without direct, firsthand research methods such as interviewing, participant observation, and/or surveying. Due to this methodological limitation, most previous work has missed many of the subtleties of the movement and instead tended to dismiss its participants as misinformed, conservative, and antifeminist. This book thus aims to supplement previous analysis and provide a more full understanding of the movement from the inside.

After years of in-depth interviewing and participant observation, I have developed a more complex understanding of this movement. Indeed, participants do use ideas from the inspirational texts, and when they do, they have some inaccurate and/or conservative views of history, mythology, and/or gender issues. However, the important thing to see is that the participants do not mindlessly internalize and follow the written texts. Most of the time, members of the movement are creatively developing meaning in the moment, drawing on a wide range of sources, and creating a discourse that is moderately liberal and that has some key feminist elements. Although the participants are clearly not as well informed about gender issues or history as many academics, this can be said of almost every social movement.

Careful analysis must reach beyond the political temptation to dismiss the movement because the participants are not progressive enough. Obviously the movement is worth serious study regardless of its political makeup. Further, instead of it being a monolithically conservative, antifeminist backlash, close analysis actually shows a very complex and subtle range of political beliefs, some of which are liberal, some of which are conservative, and some of which are quite progressive. Cultural analysis using ethnography brings out these dynamics in ways that previous studies of movement writings have been unable to do.

Before acknowledging the many sources of support for this project I have received over the years, I would like to begin by thanking Springer Science and Business Media for permission to draw some excerpts from my article in *Qualitative Sociology,* "Cultural Discourse in Action: Interactional Dynamics and Symbolic Meaning" (2005). I would also like to thank The Men's Studies Press for permission to draw some excerpts from my forthcoming article in the *Journal of Men's Studies,* "Creating Culture in the Mythopoetic Men's Movement: An Ethnographic Study of Micro-level Leadership and Socialization" (forthcoming). Lastly, I thank Sage Publications for the permission to draw some excerpts from my article in the *Journal of Contemporary Ethnography,* "Rejecting the American Dream: Men Creating Alternative Life Goals" (2007).

I would also like to thank the many people who supported me intellectually, emotionally, and/or financially throughout this project. Several mentors and colleagues were crucial in supporting this project through its multiple stages. Jeffrey Alexander has provided me with invaluable guidance and encouragement for many years. In countless ways, he has been an irreplaceable mentor who has helped me develop skills that will last a lifetime. His leadership of the reading group affectionately known as the "Culture Club" was a major contribution to my intellectual and professional growth while I was at the University of California–Los Angeles. I also thank Peter Kollock, who supported this project throughout. He provided not only specific focused feedback, but a broader perspective and enthusiasm that reminded me of the infinite potential of a life inspired by ideas. Also, Helen Deutsch's friendly, open-minded, and thoughtful support was greatly appreciated.

A number of colleagues provided me with support and guidance as I developed this project. The members of the aforementioned "Culture Club" made invaluable contributions during our many stimulating discussions. I particularly thank Christopher Campbell, Ronald Jacobs, Steven Sherwood, Andrew Roth, Eyal Rabinovitch, Anne Kane, Jennifer DeRose, Hannah Kully, John Choi, Sara Schatz, Luis Escala-Rabadan, Robert Gedeon, and Marian Katz. I also thank Benjamin Frymer and Sung Choi for their challenging ideas in the beginning stages of this project. Additionally, I thank Nicholas Wolfinger, who was an inspiration in a wide variety of ways.

Two colleagues and mentors not directly involved in the writing process itself were nonetheless pivotal in the development of this project and my larger intellectual growth. I extend heartfelt and deeply enthusiastic thanks to Carl Boggs for his friendship and unrelenting support in my greater intellectual development. His spirit and broader vision helped give this enterprise that much more meaning. Thanks also to Renee Anspach, with whom I brainstormed the original idea for this project and whose methodological teachings and inspiration were invaluable.

My research and writing were also facilitated by the material resources and assistance I received from several sources. I thank the Department of Sociology at the University of California–Los Angeles for providing me with financial support of various kinds in the beginning of this process. I thank the UCLA Center for the Study of Women for their travel support, which aided in the development of this project. Special thanks go to Marlies Dietrich, Mary Jo Johnson, and Judy Greenberg. I thank the Department of Sociology at Pomona College, especially Lynn Rapaport, for helpful support in the middle of this project. The Department of Sociology at Loyola Marymount University deserves particular thanks for providing me with important backing. For their support, I especially thank James Faught, James Mathieu, Margaret Hunter, Stacy Burns, David Marple, and Peter Hoffman. I would also like to thank my student research assistants over the years, who helped in many invaluable ways, particularly Margaret Mahoney, Nichole Ricotta, Elizabeth Fasse, Marisol Luevanos, Jamesia Brown, Maria Sotomayor, and Emily Damiells. Thanks also go to everyone at Paradigm Publishers, especially Dean Birkenkamp, Beth Davis, Melanie Stafford, and Julie Kirsch.

I thank my mother, Sharon Magnuson, for her boundless support and enthusiasm for my ongoing development. I thank my father, Peter Magnuson, for his inspiration and expansive vision. Thanks also to Marty Klein, who has been supportive throughout. Thanks additionally go to several good friends over the years, Shoshannah Boray, David Grotell, Ellen Reese, Eric Rivera, Elaine Gerber, and Peter Stamatov, who provided me with emotional sustenance, thoughtful ideas, and true friendship that helped make it all possible. I also owe a debt of gratitude to Yakkha Mackler and Zachary Van Pelt, who helped support the last stages of the project. Finally, I thank my wonderful partner, Bonnie Zucker, whose love and emotional nourishment made the closing stages of this project that much more meaningful and enjoyable.

*Eric Magnuson*

# Cultural Construction and Social Change

The mythopoetic men's movement is a fascinating and perplexing phenomenon. It has been a key part of the national soul-searching concerning gender. The movement has been a smaller part of a grand historical process that is simultaneously deeply personal and explosively political. The mythopoetic movement grew steadily from its small beginnings in the 1970s, and by the 1990s it had become a significant part of the gut-wrenching cultural and political struggle over gender identity and equality. Its success was such that it became referred to as *the* men's movement despite the existence of other important men's movements. Its most prominent leading force, Robert Bly, became a major public figure and inspiration for the movement. His *Iron John* continued to sell well after it spent more than thirty-five weeks at the top of best-seller lists in 1991. Well over one hundred thousand men have directly participated in movement activities over the years, and the number continues to grow.[1] When combined with all the individuals directly and indirectly affected by those participants, as well as the millions of people exposed to the movement through best-selling books and widespread international media coverage, the movement's effect is clearly noteworthy.

## MASCULINITY AND GENDER POLITICS

It has become commonplace within work on masculinity, and in the popular media, to refer to "the crisis of masculinity." However, it is necessary to go beyond this phrase and talk about a "crisis in gender." To do this involves acknowledging first that masculinity and femininity are constituted in each other, that they are defined in opposition to each other, both using the same broader discourse of gender and gendered identity.[2] To question and challenge femininity is to question and challenge masculinity, and vice versa. Indeed, this struggle over gender identity and power has been underway for hundreds, if not thousands, of years, most obviously in the twentieth century's first and second waves of feminism. The current cultural and political project of the reformulation of masculinity started immediately alongside the second-wave women's movement in the 1970s. Slow to start, men's participation in the questioning of hegemonic masculinity has now reached a plateau of popular energy where it is acceptable to speak broadly of a "crisis in masculinity." Men have finally joined women in confronting the still-unanswered questions in this heightened state of a "crisis in gender" at this point in early-twenty-first-century American and global history.

However, going even further, this broad gender crisis signals an ongoing cultural crisis concerning the very nature of society itself. The women's movement has always had as its goal a fundamental reworking of society. Even the moderate/liberal side of the movement has consistently worked for widespread change in all institutions of our society: the economy and workplace, the family, the political system, education, religion, and the media. In short, every aspect of life, public and private, is being challenged.

It is this context into which the mythopoetic men's movement steps. While there are certainly conservative components to this movement, its progressive elements will contribute to the continuing history of social change of which it is a part. This movement's liberal, progressive elements have shown their cultural vitality and popularity in the larger society. For instance, surprisingly, many movement participants share an overarching ideological vision with radical feminism: that Western society is at its foundation a masculine society and that both women and men suffer because of this. What the mythopoetic men's movement adds is a new critique of the fundamental ways in which men (and women) suffer emotionally under hegemonic masculine culture. The primary focus of the movement is on masculinity, to be sure, but a progressive, counterhegemonic vision is one of the foundations of the entire movement.

The movement is in a liminal space in the middle of an identity crisis of masculinity (and of gender in general). In responding to the women's movement, the participants agree that traditional, hegemonic masculinity has to be changed. However, they generally disagree with the liberal feminist position that the solution lies in finding some kind of moderate gender identity through the simultaneous rejection of the extremes of masculinity and the extremes of femininity. They also disagree with certain radical feminist arguments that the entire project of masculinity is the fundamental problem. Thus they generally reject gender moderation and androgyny, and they rule out the idea of reformulating the world in a solely feminine image. Rather, they often side with another radical feminist perspective, namely, that men and women are, at an essential level, inherently different and that the best in both must be radically brought forth as a solution to the current gender identity crisis. The real issue for these men becomes that of constructing this new masculinity, one that is not traditionally feminine, traditionally masculine, or androgynous. Thus, these men are part of an organized, sustained identity creation movement. It is a microcosm of the historical process of the reformulation of gender and, thus, of Western culture overall. It is a seed movement, crystallizing a new model of masculinity and creating new possibilities for the culture at large.

To be more specific, the men hold a general belief in the traditionally feminine qualities of emotional openness, intimacy, love, supportiveness, trust, and creativity. However, they simultaneously celebrate what are seen as the essential qualities of maleness: adventurousness, assertiveness, strength, power, criticalness, and directness. These latter qualities are seen as in some way inherently male. It is an open question how exactly women fit into this schema. They are generally seen as inherently gifted in the traditional feminine abilities listed above and as inherently weaker in the more traditionally masculine abilities. However, all of these qualities are coded as fundamentally positive regardless of gender, so women are generally expected to have some of these traditionally masculine qualities as well. It is a curious position politically, conservative and antifeminist in some ways, yet progressive and feminist in others.

The movement has no publicly stated, "official" position on these gender issues. There are men who tend more in the direction of the androgyny ideal, focused on creating a blended identity that is a combination of the best of both genders. However, there are also men who tend more in the direction of the essentialist vision of inherent difference, where men can and should "specialize" in the more masculine side and women can and should "specialize" in the feminine side. While these issues will become much clearer in the analysis in the following chapters of this book, it is safe to conclude for now that the men of the movement generally believe in what has been called a "loose essentialism" (Schwalbe 1996). They draw on essentialist ideas of gender from time to time, but generally they see gender as perfectible and socially constructed, something that can, and must, be changed from its traditional form. They believe that the future of society depends in part on the outcome of this struggle.

## THE MYTHOPOETIC MEN'S MOVEMENT

So what exactly *is* this strange social movement? It has been a major force in American society that has produced widespread media coverage, best-selling books, and countless lecture and workshop tours. Across the country, therapists and other mythopoetic leaders have offered workshops, retreats, and seminars meant to construct new masculinities that reincorporate traditional and/or archetypal masculine forms into the newer forms that have grown out of the modern social and cultural context. The movement is self-consciously motivated toward identifying and repairing what are seen as the damages to men, women, and children caused by missing fathers, by overtaxed and misled mothers, by psychologically damaging workplace environments, and by what is seen as a general culture that has become overly materialistic and spiritually lacking.

The movement has always been a relatively decentralized national phenomenon that is based primarily on the small-group consciousness-raising model. Individual local groups are generally composed of between five and fifteen men and are usually facilitated and organized by men with prior experience in the movement and/or professional therapy experience. Generally the members pay the leaders a relatively low fee, using a sliding scale based on ability to pay, with the idea that no one is turned away for financial reasons. Complementing these small, local organizations has been a myriad of workshops, retreats, campouts, speaker events, and other organized activities that occur across the nation. Further feeding the movement are popular books, articles, and audio recordings that help bring new members into the movement and motivate existing members.

During group meetings, the men generally sit in a circle on chairs and open each meeting with drumming, chanting, and/or some form of meditation. The majority of the meeting is usually spent in free-form discussion of personal issues raised by the men. The meetings generally last between one and a half to two and a half hours and are then followed by informal individual conversations afterward. Friendships are formed that bring men together outside of formal events.

The men are self-consciously interested in coming together, as men, to explore their personal identities and to grow emotionally and spiritually. They come to the movement in reaction to an outside world that they see as not taking these concerns seriously, a world in which they feel that they are expected to perform, work hard, and succeed but are not encouraged to feel, share, and explore personal growth. They come to discuss other men and the various relationships that they have with them, and they come to discuss problems with romantic relationships with their partners, problems with communication and love. These men, on the whole, tend to see their groups as places where these issues can be explored in great depth, where they can "let their walls down," and where they can feel safe to expose what they see as their "inner selves." Ultimately, members of these groups see themselves as being on a path of self-discovery and growth that leads to their greater maturity, empowerment, and ability to love and share. To varying degrees, these men aim to help create what they see as a better world, starting with their immediate personal relationships with their partners, children, male friends, mothers, fathers, other family members, coworkers, and more. They feel that they have been let down by a framework of masculinity that does not let them express and develop their "true selves" and that limits and damages them emotionally and spiritually.

The men are explicitly oriented toward constructing new forms of masculinity through criticizing what they see as the dominant or hegemonic form that they feel has limited them throughout their lives. They are consciously trying to remake themselves and to remake gender ideology. The men often share extremely intense emotions and actively negotiate the meaning of events and actions in their lives. Group-level interaction is thus an effective site to explore the ideological construction, negotiation, and contestation that is a central day-to-day part of the movement. Detailed, long-term participant observation research is a key entry point into the complicated processes of making manifest this unusual social movement.

The mythopoetic movement has certainly been a flash point of political debate. It has been widely criticized, from caricatured, ridiculing portraits in the popular media to more reasoned analysis on the part of feminist critics. Haunting the movement has been images of middle- and upper-middle-class white men wildly chanting and dancing naked around bonfires, bonding as they complain about their wives, girlfriends, mothers, and fathers.[3] The feminist portrait of the mythopoetic men's movement is sometimes of a self-serving clan of antifeminist white men trying to defend their waning patriarchal privileges. Upon close analysis, it becomes clear that these visions are, at best, only partially accurate, and at worst they are crude stereotypes, generally based on little or no direct observation. Surprisingly, hardly any discussion of the movement, whether critical or not, has come from direct empirical social scientific analysis. Thus, one of the contributions of this book is to shed serious analytical light on the motivations and actions of the movement's participants by examining closely the content of their ideological constructions and their corresponding behavior outside the movement context. It is important to answer carefully the question of what this movement is actually doing in terms of moral, cultural, and political ideals and what its real effects are on these men's lives and the lives of others.

One of the points of debate concerning this movement has been its racial, class, and, of course, gender makeup. Certainly the demographics of the movement are one of its many curious features. Almost all of its participants are white, relatively well educated, and middle, upper-middle, or upper class. They are generally heterosexual and between thirty-five and sixty years old. These features provide a sense of who makes up this movement, but it does not explain *why* these particular men have joined. For this, it is helpful to look at the common motivations and cultural beliefs that brought them to the movement. These are men who have had the opportunity to step outside the mainstream cultural beliefs of their society. By the time they join the movement, they have already developed some critical understanding of what they see as the dominant culture. Their motivation to become part of the movement stems from their desire to explore alternative ways of thinking and ways of living that might address their doubts about the mainstream society of which they had been a part.

On a fundamental level, these men have succeeded in life according to traditional definitions and using traditional paths. They have gotten a respectable education, they have professional careers, and they are financially stable and successful. However, they consistently report being motivated to join the movement because of some lack of satisfaction with their lives, despite having generally achieved and developed the characteristics that they have been told will bring them happiness.

This dynamic is one of the most interesting features of the movement: the members are not arguing for inclusion, as in many social movements. They do not contend that they have been discriminated against and excluded for some reason such as race, gender, class, or sexual orientation. Indeed, they generally have every identity characteristic that can be said to be valued in American society. Thus their critique of hegemonic masculinity and American culture more broadly is all the more interesting *precisely because* it comes from a standpoint of success. They do not seek inclusion and success on the existing terms of society; rather, they already have traditional success and identify it as empty, unfulfilling, alienating, and destructive in certain ways. They ultimately want to change the fundamental goals and values on which the culture is founded, not simply tinker with how to achieve those goals and values. In this sense there is a significant progressive aspect to their project. Instead of a traditionally liberal vision of balancing out men's and women's relative power *within the existing system,* they seek to change the overall system itself. This overlaps in a small yet interesting way with the progressive feminist position that instead of fighting for women to achieve in terms of men's goals of gaining money and power, those very goals and thus the very cultural system should be changed away from the valuing of money and power in the first place. This is a curious dynamic, given that mythopoetic men's politics, as traditionally defined, are on the whole moderately liberal. Later analysis shows this unusual dynamic to be a very significant cultural and political phenomenon. It can tell us much about specific aspects of our contemporary culture as well as suggest new ways of understanding culture in general.

## PREVIOUS UNDERSTANDINGS OF THE MOVEMENT

The ethnographic approach used here fills in gaps left by previous research, which has tended to focus on the writings of movement leaders rather than the actions of actual participants. Previous research has only rarely looked at the social construction of meaning on the interactional level. The primary reason is methodological: scholars have almost entirely confined themselves to analyzing the published writings of movement leaders, thereby underappreciating what grassroots members actually think and do (e.g., Clatterbaugh 1997; Connell 1995, 2005; Kimmel 1996; Kimmel and Kaufman 1994; Messner 1997; Newton 2005). Rather than conduct participant observation or interview research, these scholars have almost entirely limited themselves to textual analysis of major mythopoetic writers. As shown by Bartkowski (2000, 2002, 2003), incomplete understandings of men's movement beliefs and actions are often the result when scholars focus only on the writings of elite leaders; there is an implicit assumption that members simply follow the beliefs of the popular writers. This is a clear methodological weakness because the accuracy of this assumption cannot be determined without microlevel research. My research shows that participants do not unreflectively internalize the ideas of writers. In fact, in the discussions of men's group participants, they generally pay small attention to the published texts and often have read few or none of them. Close ethnographic research reveals that the grassroots members are significantly more creative and independent in their thinking and actions than much previous scholarship suggests. Members innovate and create in the lived moment of interaction, often diverting significantly from the beliefs and suggestions of movement leaders and writers.

A second reason that previous work has overlooked many issues concerning the social construction of meaning within the movement is that it has tended to focus on creating a political critique of the movement. The motivation has generally been to criticize the movement from a feminist perspective. The movement writings are picked apart and dismissed in terms of their gender ideology being overly conservative and antifeminist. While I am certainly sympathetic to the political standpoint of these analyses, their focus on movement writings tends to miss the complex political culture of the movement itself. In fact, the political ideology of the movement is internally contradictory and variable, including ideas that are liberal, conservative, and progressive. Overall, the movement is best described as being moderately liberal.[4] Further, these analyses tend not to explore sufficiently the aspects of the movement that do not concern gender issues. While it is a men's movement, it is about more than masculinity and gender. Focused in these ways, previous scholarship often overlooks the extent to which the men of this movement are constructing a critique of a range of mainstream cultural beliefs. Among other progressive ideas, the men actively criticize an overdeveloped interest in the accumulation of money and achievement of professional prestige. As a result, previous work has generally missed the ways in which these men are changing their lives in corresponding ways as an outcome of their participation in the movement.

It is the few studies that have used interviews and/or participant observation (e.g., Barton 2000; Schwalbe 1995, 1996) that have been able to avoid these limitations of other research.[5] While certainly pointing out the movement's weaknesses, work using these research methods has also been able to explore some of the complex ways in which men are creatively changing their ideas and behavior and criticizing the mainstream culture. This book builds on their findings by bringing to bear a new perspective: cultural sociology, combined with an interest in power and hegemony, using ethnographic methods.

## HEGEMONY, DISCOURSE, AND THE AMERICAN DREAM

Applying and developing new ideas from cultural sociology makes it possible to understand the mythopoetic men's movement in new ways.

Specifically, it is useful to explore and apply new, culturally robust understandings of ideological construction and cultural discourse that include a fully cultural notion of hegemony and, more particularly, hegemonic masculinity. Developing a new form of cultural ethnography, this study examines the dynamics of ideological construction and hegemony.

The first of three major points of analysis in the study is to examine, at the micro level, how dynamics of power and socialization operate within the core context of the movement, the individual men's group. Here the specific focus is on the role of the group facilitator as an organic intellectual (in the Gramscian sense). Using his authority, the leader guides the social construction of cultural discourse. The group facilitator is self-consciously an activist in the larger men's movement. He is very directive and mission-oriented, developing a top-down structure of power and guidance. While it is at times contested and undermined and is never totally effective, his power is nonetheless quite effective at cultural/political construction. The facilitator constantly works as a socialization agent, suggesting, persuading, manipulating, and cajoling. He creates rules and is the primary maintainer of local norms. He selects group members in order that they will become active participants, joining the movement as dedicated activists.

The group leader also has the power to suggest, pressure, or demand that people leave the group if he feels they are not "working out," that is, if they are not fulfilling his ideals of the group culture. The facilitator actively works to transfer the ideology of the movement as he sees it through several key practices that are explored in depth later in the book. Of course this process is far from perfectly smooth. The conflict and negotiation that is a fundamental part of this process serves as the window through which to see the internal ideological dynamics involved, including contestation, disagreement, repression, negotiation, compromise, and contradiction.

Through these processes, members actively internalize aspects of the ideology, making it their own. They become true members of the movement, no longer seeing themselves as entering a movement that is other than them. This is particularly central because the movement is itself about personal identity and emotional makeup. Members come to identify the movement and themselves as one and the same. It is not something they *do*; it becomes something they *are*.

In addition to examining the *process* of social construction, a second major focus of this book is to examine the *content* of it. Specifically, the question is how the members of the movement construct and negotiate images of hegemonic masculinity and hegemonic culture and, simultaneously, counterhegemonic masculinity and counterhegemonic culture. The members of the movement explicitly see themselves as reacting to a dominant form of masculinity that they view as having limited and damaged them emotionally and spiritually throughout their lives. This dominant form of identity is conceived of herein as hegemonic masculinity. Further "culturalizing" the concept of hegemony, the analysis examines how hegemonic masculinity is seen as restricting and suppressing alternative masculinities. The members of the movement do the cultural work of constructing their own specific structured discourse of hegemonic masculinity and simultaneously constructing a discourse of counterhegemonic masculinity. The men see themselves as judged through, and in explicit competition through, the evaluative framework of this dominant discourse of masculinity. It is this complex system of restriction and limitation that these men report, and it is the formulating of a counterhegemonic masculinity that is their personal and political project within the movement.

The third major focus of this book is the analysis of how the men of the movement critique what they see as a dominant cultural theme, the American work ethic and the American Dream. This book contributes to the discussion of the gender aspects of the movement but also broadens the focus to include a central, but deeply underappreciated, aspect of the movement, the critique of modernity, rationalization, and the culture of capitalism. The group members develop a critical understanding of what they see as a destructive cultural emphasis on traditional professional achievement and material accumulation. Having constructed this vision, they then change their lives outside of the movement to opt out of this aspect of American culture. The gender critique discussed earlier and this larger cultural critique are two sides of the same ideological coin. Close empirical analysis shows that the men conceive of hegemonic masculinity as complicit in the maintenance of a cultural system that prioritizes economic productivity and hard work over the ideals of emotional happiness, love, and spirituality. It is a critique that is interestingly similar to some forms of radical feminism, but one that is certainly developed in a unique way by these men.

The members of the movement particularly focus on the psychological toll of the traditional role of man-as-provider. The men criticize the emotional price of the modern life path of professional success and material achievement. In a curious and unique way, these men are undermining the very cultural logic that has brought them the many rewards they enjoy in their lives. They are the victors in a hierarchical social system, yet at the very moment of their success they trumpet major flaws of that very system. In this strange way, they seem to contradict their own class interests.

A central premise of the movement is that men's groups and other mythopoetic events are meant to result in not simply discussion but real social change (albeit on a relatively individualistic level). The men take their critical understanding outside of the movement context, applying it to their own social worlds. They create at times dramatic changes in their lives and the lives of many others. The realization of these life alterations is in part the "payoff" of the movement. In other words, these changes are key sites at which the movement clearly has discernable effects on the larger social world. Each participant spreads new ideas and new behaviors to the many people in his own life. As he affects others, they too affect others in their lives, and the process continues, like ripples in a pond. One can imagine well over one hundred thousand points of impact, each point sending out a cycle of ripples. Add this to the media directly produced by the movement and the mainstream media coverage of the movement, and a significant social impact is created. It is in these myriad ways that the mythopoetic men's movement effects the larger dynamics of social change in American society.[6]

## CULTURAL SOCIOLOGY, POWER, AND ETHNOGRAPHY

This study aims to make two contributions to the larger study of this social phenomenon. It does this primarily by attempting to develop in two major new directions the strong program of cultural sociology in the Alexander tradition.[7] One of these contributions is the inclusion of power and hegemony; the other is the incorporation of ethnography and microlevel analysis. Both of these are new to this strand of cultural analysis, which has long been criticized as not being able to fully analyze both power and agency (just as functionalism has been accurately criticized since the 1950s).

First, my approach combines cultural sociology with Marxist theory, specifically cultural Marxism and the Gramscian tradition. My analysis lays out the actual discourse and transformational culture within men's movement contexts but looks at this as a form of rebellion against power. Thus, the organic intellectuals of the movement are applying the social change ideas of the movement high intellectuals in order to create and mobilize a political movement. They are instilling a new counterhegemonic vision among the population in order to ultimately change the social order. The theoretical model thus shows how organic intellectuals actually change intellectual hegemony in the lived reality of cultural interpretation and meaning construction.

Hegemony can be seen as pure power that is legitimized and made authoritative through microcultural interpretive techniques. In this way, all cultural life is filled with the exercise of power, which is negotiated inside the meaning system but draws from sources outside the system. These sources can be cultural, for instance from the larger men's movement and its networks. They can also be material, such as the authority of office or wealth.

Synthesizing cultural sociology with Marxist theory allows the understanding of power and domination in a way that does not reduce culture to the outcome of mechanistic determinants. Thus, meaning can be seen as relatively autonomous in terms of its causal role, but power and inequality can be incorporated as well. This helps avoid the trap of idealism that has haunted cultural work throughout its history.

The second major contribution to cultural sociology that my work attempts to make is to show how ethnography can be used as a research method in order to better understand the construction of culture in contingent, face-to-face interaction. More specifically, the study uses long-term, longitudinal ethnography in the structural analysis of culture. This is new to ethnography in that the study of interaction is almost always kept to the micro level, with conclusions rarely made concerning larger cultural issues on a more macro or structural level. This is also new to cultural sociology, which has tended to use archival sources in its research. Thus, this book shows how a close analysis of everyday talk, over long periods in a focused setting with close attention to significant interactions, can bring the strong program of cultural sociology to the micro level in a very productive way. This approach can generate new understandings of how culture is created and changed by active individuals in creative interaction. This contributes to the larger development of micro-macro synthesis, making the connection between analytical realms that have traditionally been divided both theoretically and methodologically.

### GETTING INSIDE THE MYTHOPOETIC MOVEMENT

This book is an in-depth, longitudinal ethnography, conducted over the span of eight years from the mid-1990s into the new millennium. Given the significant length of time of the research, I was able to concretely verify the validity of the findings as well as observe change over time, seeing the longer-term effects of the movement on individual men and seeing the development and application of the movement ideology. Longitudinal ethnography is a rare methodology because of the length of time required to carry it out. However, it is especially effective because the data have a temporal component that deepens the analysis in highly productive ways. The specific research methods I employed are participant observation in group meetings; informal discussions with members before and after meetings and via telephone; in-depth, open-ended field interviews in person and by telephone; participant observation at campouts, retreats, and workshops; and textual analysis of the major mythopoetic publications. Specifically, I attended about 230 meetings, conducted about 55 hours of interviews, attended 3 weekend campouts and 12 workshops, and engaged in probably 600–700 informal conversations.

I was not able to take detailed notes during most of the mythopoetic events because I had to remain unobtrusive. No real researcher role is available during the group meetings and most other events, so anything beyond rudimentary note taking was impossible. Instead, I wrote up condensed handwritten field notes immediately after events. On such occasions I would leave the immediate vicinity of the event and commit the notes to paper. This made it possible to record observations as soon as possible after the activities occurred while still being separate from the participants. I also entered field notes into a computer database immediately upon return from an event.

One important issue was my role as researcher. I did not have any problem becoming a trusted confidant of members of these groups. In fact, I actually became a fully legitimate member of the movement in a fairly brief time. The group participants brought this about through their conscious, concerted effort to incorporate new people into the movement. This degree of trust was clearly a very positive development for the research.

However, the interesting issue was that there was little social space for a researcher to be anything *but* a full member. This is the opposite of the usual problem of gaining the confidence of the members. At the outset of the research, I informed organizers that I wanted to conduct sociological research on the proceedings, and I was never denied entrée. However, I was instructed on several occasions not to mention my researcher role immediately in order for the men to get to know me on a personal level. It was made clear to me that I must be a member first and an academic observer second. As part of this, I was instructed not to "act like a researcher" on the grounds that it would break down the cohesion of the group context and set me apart from the other men. As soon as it seemed appropriate, I would then make my research identity known to the participants. The only exception to this was at large campouts or workshops where it was impractical to make every single participant aware of my identity. In this case, I only used specific individual data from an individual if he had provided informed consent to be part of the study.

The challenge of this arrangement was that it was often impossible to fully utilize a researcher role with the men themselves. For instance, at group events I had to engage in discussion and activities as a full participant. In this way I could influence the very phenomenon that I was observing. The threat of a Hawthorne effect was significant, although this fundamental dynamic is a challenge in any research of this type. In order to address this challenge, I was careful not to be an unusual participant in any movement activity. For instance, I avoided suggesting new directions or disagreeing with standard, established procedures. Thus I tried to ascertain what kind of behavior was in some sense "average" and "normal" and approximate that behavior as much as was possible and practically necessary.

Another important issue is that of confidentiality. I have given all individuals and groups pseudonyms. In addition, information that could possibly be used to identify specific individuals or groups has been altered somewhat when necessary in order to avoid the revelation of exact identity. When changes have been made, they have been almost always minor and were chosen in order to maintain the general accuracy of the overall information. In the groups many men revealed extremely personal information about themselves, making this a particularly important methodological issue. All men discussed individually in this book consented to being included in the sample and were assured of confidentiality.

The core site for the project was the Open Plain Men's Circle, located in a major metropolitan area in the United States. This organization encompassed three mythopoetic men's groups started and run by Watani, the "facilitator/firetender," as he refers to himself. By the end of this research project, the organization was over ten years old. Two of the three groups each met one night a week from roughly 7:30 p.m. to 10:00 p.m. The third group met every other week, also for about two and a half hours. Watani is a professional therapist, and he charges fees on a sliding scale based on a member's income. Most members pay twenty to twenty-five dollars per group session. Throughout the years of the study membership fluctuated, but there were generally about eight to twelve men in each group. Some men had already been members for years; others joined during the study. I also participated in other individual groups as well as numerous men's campouts, retreats, and workshops, which helped augment the primary group data.

The Open Plain Men's Circle was a specific, strategic site for my research because it is representative of what is consistently identified as the core features of the broader mythopoetic men's movement. The beliefs and practices of the men in this study were typical of the larger national movement, as apparent from reading newsletters from around the country and from talking to men who had been members of the movement in different parts of the state and different parts of the country. In talking with men who had substantial experience in different geographically located mythopoetic contexts it became clear that the differences between groups were relatively minor. For instance, some groups might do more or less drumming, have slightly different balances of the common spiritual traditions utilized, or use structured rituals in a slightly different proportion to open-ended dialogue. Nonetheless, these differences were superficial. All the evidence suggests that the ideological, cultural dynamics are fundamentally similar between the contexts in this study and the other national contexts. This is certainly to be expected, given that groups across the country draw largely on the same nationally available books, articles, and audio recordings and take their lead generally from the same national leaders who tour the country leading workshops and lecture events. While it is important to acknowledge the variation between mythopoetic contexts, it is just as important to understand that, given the focus of this research, these relatively surface differences do not entail variation at a level significant for this study.

## WHAT IS MASCULINITY?

Defining masculinity is a tricky business, but it is worthwhile as one final point of discussion here. There have been four main trajectories in defining masculinity. While these approaches can be analytically isolated, they are often combined in actual practice. Current concepts of masculinity are historical, cultural products, and recent ones at that. Gender concepts have developed throughout history, but the primary features of the current forms have emerged in only the past few hundred years. Regardless, most definitions have simply taken the current cultural standpoint for granted. In fact, to invoke the term "masculinity" at all is to necessarily be "doing gender" in a way specific to our cultural place and historical moment.

The four central types of definitions of masculinity are essentialist, positivist, normative, and semiotic. (This study utilizes a variation on the semiotic.) Essentialist definitions attempt to select personal characteristics that define the perceived core of the masculine and then tie them to biological differences between male and female, ultimately appealing to ahistorical, physical characteristics, often tied to evolutionary frameworks. The fundamental flaw of essentialist definitions of masculinity is that the choice of essence (inherent characteristics) is arbitrary, reflecting the beliefs of the interpreter rather than some independent, objective truth. Another clear weakness is that an essential core is, by definition, unchanging, and therefore gender identity and ideology cannot be fully understood as socially constructed and varying by culture and historical period.

Positivist definitions of masculinity are a second type that ultimately fails. Positivist approaches simplistically define masculinity as what men actually are in objective, observed reality. This has a number of inherent weaknesses. One is that, as contemporary epistemology holds, every description comes from a particular standpoint. The purportedly objective descriptions are actually founded in preanalytical assumptions about gender. Another weakness is that individuals must already be categorized and labeled "men" and "women" in order to empirically describe what men and women do. As explored by Kessler and McKenna (1978), this means that the categories of male and female are already written into the research before it starts, making the "discovery" of those categories tautological and meaningless. Finally, if this empirically based definition is used, one cannot analyze how some women have aspects of masculinity as part of their gender identity and some men have aspects of femininity. Positivist definitions prevent us from looking at contradictions within identity, psychoanalytically or otherwise. In fact, if solely biological men and solely biological women, as two distinct groups, are used to define masculinity and femininity, the terms are not necessary in the first place. "Male" and "female" would suffice. The very concepts of "man" and "woman" themselves necessitate the ability to analyze the ways in which men differ from other men and women differ from other women in matters of gender.

Normative definitions declare that masculine is what men ought to be. This approach is used in orthodox sex role theory and often in media studies where male role models, such as John Wayne, Mel Gibson, or Arnold Schwarzenegger, are analyzed. This approach offers some key lessons, although it ultimately falls to a number of flawed paradoxes. For instance, given the set of extreme characteristics this sort of definition commonly generates as defining masculinity, only a small minority of actual men end up embodying them. Thus, the analysis is forced to conclude that most men are unmasculine. Inevitable analytical problems arise from within this system; for example, normative definitions make it impossible to analyze a man who is a gay football hero or a take-no-prisoners crusader for women's rights. There are some theoretical moves that can be made to avoid these problems, but they generally constitute a shift toward the semiotic definition (discussed next). On a more subtle level, a purely normative definition offers little analytical power with respect to masculinity at the level of personality. Role and identity are generally conflated, as discussed by Pleck (1976). These various internal confusions may suggest why practitioners of this approach frequently draw on essentialism to underpin their work, although often do so apparently unwittingly.

It is the semiotic definition and approach that is used to build the analysis in this study. In this approach, masculinity is understood as a structured, symbolic system based in difference. Masculinity is the opposite of femininity, and vice versa. The semiotic definition is intrinsically relational, and it is common in poststructuralist cultural work, feminist scholarship, Lacanian psychoanalysis, linguistics, and comparative literature. Masculinity is seen in the larger culture as the unmarked term, that is, the presumably neutral site of authority on the symbolic level. Femininity is symbolically defined and evaluated by absence, as that which does not have masculinity, which does not embody the phallus, which is the other. This definition is free of the arbitrary and biological focus of essentialism while at the same time it avoids the inherent internal contradictions of positivist and normative definitions.[8]

The definition of masculinity I use in this book is a synthesis of the semiotic approach and late Durkheimian and Parsonian cultural sensitivities. Thus, masculinities can be understood not as free-floating symbolic structures but as constituted in very real ways in individual consciousness through affective ties. Masculinities are internalized through interaction and emotional attachment. Thus, through complex processes of socialization, individuals internalize, to varying degrees, different aspects of masculinity. Any individual man's consciousness is a mixture of a number of elements of masculinity that importantly help constitute his identity as a social being. Thus, masculinities are structured, symbolic systems (which will be analyzed as discourses) that are a macroproduct of historical development through specific, microsituated interaction. Masculinities are socially constructed yet transcend the control of any one individual at any one time.

## OUTLINE OF THE BOOK

Chapter 2 explores some major theoretical issues involved in the study of masculinity. Selected previous work on the topic is reviewed to ascertain the strengths and weaknesses of the literature and establish the major dynamics that are dealt with in later chapters. The existing research in the area of masculinity offers a number of lessons that constitute the starting point of this project.

Chapter 3 specifically targets the movement on a micro level, exploring the processes of social construction that go into the interactional development of the cultural discourse of the movement. The chapter examines the role of the local leader in the small group context and explores his place as an ideological agent contributing to the moral and political vision of the movement. My analysis explores how the leader acts as an organic intellectual in the Gramscian sense, presenting and interpreting the works of the movement high intellectuals. The leader is a key socializing agent, consciously acting as an ideological guide to steer the men toward movement beliefs and values, and my analysis shows a number of specific interactional practices that the leader uses.

Chapter 4 takes an in-depth look at the master discourse of the movement, the discourse of mythopoetic masculinity. Over time the men construct a complex, structured understanding of what they see as hegemonic masculinity versus counterhegemonic masculinity. My analysis progressively maps out the discourse in terms of its complex binary structure. The men report that they have been unwittingly socialized into the hegemonic form of masculinity, which they feel has limited and damaged them throughout their lives. The primary goal of the movement is to replace this form of masculinity with the liberational form. In this sense, the movement is very much premised on the consciousness-raising model of second-wave feminism. The members construct the hegemonic code as constituted in the profane characteristics of being unreliable, overly rational, disempowered, emotionally closed off, deceitful, unloving, competitive, and oppressive. They simultaneously construct the sacred code of liberational masculinity as constituted in the binary opposite, positive characteristics of being reliable, spiritual, open-minded, empowered, emotionally open, truthful, loving, cooperative, and liberational.

Chapter 5 examines another central aspect of the mythopoetic movement's cultural project, the critique of what they see as the American work ethic. The men construct an understanding of American culture as featuring a dominant belief in work, professional achievement, and material success. The analysis exposes on a detailed level how they develop this critique, mobilizing a specific mythopoetic version of the neo-Weberian critique of the culture of capitalism and rationalization. The men then apply these ideas directly to their lives, often deciding to lower the priority of professional achievement and raise the priority of family, love, personal pursuits, and spirituality. Often this involves difficult decisions to lower career goals, change jobs, accept a lower salary, and/or have less social prestige. It is an individualistic solution, but one they hope will gradually change society through the diffusion of counterhegemonic values. The longitudinal ethnographic data make it possible to analyze a number of case studies of individual men who have made significant and sometimes dramatic changes over the period of several years in the movement.

Chapter 6 concludes the analysis, stepping back to review the major findings of the study and suggesting ways in which its theoretical and empirical contributions can be applied in future work.

## NOTES

1. In the mid-1990s, the level of participation was widely estimated at one hundred thousand (Schwalbe 1996).

2. In semiotic terms, they are a binary pair dependent on each other for meaning (Saussure 1985). Thus, there cannot be a change in one without a change in the other. It is this basic relationship that underlies the historical fact that the current men's movements have a reactive relationship to the women's movement. It becomes clear that a crisis in masculinity cannot exist without there being a crisis in femininity.

3. See Kimmel and Kaufman (1994) for further discussion of this criticism of the movement.

4. For instance, although I did not gather quantitative data on this point, it is very clear from my research that Democrats strongly outnumbered Republicans among the participants studied. Interestingly, on many occasions I observed men teasing or criticizing a Republican for his political beliefs whereas I rarely observed the opposite. Republicans were almost always outnumbered and opposed whenever they voiced clearly conservative political positions.

5. See Karides (1998) for a discussion of the strengths of Schwalbe's (1996) ethnographic research.

6. The number of active movement participants has declined over the past few years. However, the movement still has strong local groups that are well-institutionalized and continue to attract new participants (Fox 2004).

7. For a recent statement of Alexander's conception of the strong program in cultural sociology, see Alexander (2003).

8. For more on these issues, see Connell (1995).

## 2

# A New Direction in Interpreting Masculinity

Most social science is about men, but it is the analysis of masculinity itself that is more recent (Morgan 1981). The study of masculinity is one of several new directions in not only the study of gender but the social sciences as a whole. Through theoretical development and empirical analysis, the field is challenging many long-standing paradigms and divisions within social science. Simultaneously, new studies of masculinity are exploring aspects of the empirical world that have remained hidden due to the limitations of previous perspectives.

Fully understanding masculinity requires an understanding of how culture works in the creation, maintenance, and change of gender ideology. Gender studies, and masculinity studies in particular, is benefiting from the "cultural turn" in social sciences that allows a more complex understanding of the dynamics of meaning that constitute gender as both an identity and a site of political struggle. Cultural sociology offers a body of conceptual tools that can be used to understand these phenomena in ways impossible with older, traditional approaches.

The history of the study of masculinity has proceeded through three dominant paradigms: the psychological/Freudian paradigm, the sex role/functionalist paradigm, and, finally, the new set of interdisciplinary social science approaches. The older psychological and functionalist paradigms each offer lessons for current study but must ultimately be rejected as conceptual frameworks. The new social science approaches offer true promise for the development of the field. In particular, I present a new cultural sociology approach useful to empirical analysis that will be shown later in detail. I uncover the ways in which masculinity can be studied in a fully cultural way, incorporating the role of culture structures while at the same time bringing together the understanding of contingency, interaction, power, conflict, and social change.

## CENTRAL ISSUES IN THE STUDY OF MASCULINITY

A foundational premise of this book, as in most recent studies of masculinity, is a fundamental appreciation of the gender/sex dichotomy. A central understanding of feminist work on gender, this delineation marks *sex* as referring to the biological category of male or female and *gender* as referring to socially constructed categories of masculinity and femininity. *Gender* thus refers to a fully cultural notion of identity, released from the baggage of biological determinism and essentialism. In simple terms, gender is the product of culture, sex the product of biology; gender is the result of how one is "nurtured" or socialized, and sex is the product of "nature" (Ortner 1974; Rubin 1975; Strathern 1980).

The gender/sex dichotomy makes it possible to use concepts such as gender ideology and gendered identity. Correspondingly, I will use the term *masculinity* to refer to a gendered identity, to the set of ideas, feelings, beliefs, ideology, and related behaviors that is socially constructed through history and through the individual life course and loosely associated with the male biological sex. There is, therefore, an infinite possible variety and number of masculinities—at least as many empirical masculinities at any one time as there are actual men alive, since each individual can be understood to be unique. But for analytical purposes, we can see that certain features are shared by many men, making it possible to employ a kind of typology of masculinities. Any empirical man can be understood as incorporating into his own identity many different strands of masculinities, which will then interact in ways that can be studied further. (Of course femininity and femininities can be defined in the same way.) It becomes important for research to explore the relationships between men, relationships studied in terms of the internal point of view of men themselves as well as in terms of the more easily observed social outcomes of these relationships.

Developing more cultural approaches, masculinity work (as part of a larger development) has been able to explore the complex ways in which masculinity (and identity more broadly) is in part constituted in macrolevel, cultural structures of gender ideology. Correspondingly, the literature has begun to explore how individuals can challenge, negotiate, and change the very gender structures that have preceded them and in part constituted their own gender identities. It is an ongoing process, with this change-oriented activity deeply affected and directed by macro cultural structures, which themselves are being challenged and altered through individual action. The simplistic notion of free will within certain macrodetermined, external boundaries can be jettisoned, and the dichotomous framework that has plagued previous analysis is being increasingly transcended. In this regard, the development of the field of masculinity studies parallels the larger development of a fully dialectical understanding of identity, culture, and social change, a fundamental, underlying challenge that has yet to be fully resolved by social science.

A closely related direction of development in work on masculinity deals with power, social change, resistance, opposition, and the ideal/material dichotomy. Masculinity work generally takes as a starting point the empirical observation of power difference between men and women in general. While it is clearly important to study this in economic ways, it is increasingly studied in terms of cultural and emotional dynamics, such as in sexual relationships or in the workplace. While power difference in terms of gender is generally studied as a dynamic *between* men and women, it is increasingly also studied as a dynamic *within* genders, that is, between men and men or women and women. Power and material inequality is often analyzed in terms of the ways in which it is constituted in ideas and, more specifically, the ways in which it is constituted in ideology. (Here *ideology* is being used in the Geertzian [1973] sense.) Further, beliefs can be examined in terms of how they are shaped and changed through material causality. The interpenetration of ideational dynamics and material dynamics can thus be studied in more sophisticated ways than previously possible. Ultimately, the material and the ideal can be seen as two sides of the same coin, related and changing in dialectical ways that have yet to be fully explored by social science.

The study of social change within masculinity work has correspondingly become more sophisticated. The prevalent social order at any given time is seen as a product of and open to contestation, negotiation, resistance, and opposition. Thus interaction is increasingly studied as an ongoing process of agreement, disagreement, challenge, compliance, defiance, misunderstanding, compromise, tension, and so on. Taking a cue from microperspectives, the social order can be seen as being constantly reinvented, whether on the scale of the seconds of a personal interaction or hundreds of years of history. Incorporating insights from conflict theory, interaction and gender identity can be seen as a constant site of struggle, whether overt, conscious, and easily observed or internal, unconscious, and difficult to study directly. One significant advancement along these lines is the move from studying differences between men and women to studying relations between them. Relations can change through their own internal dynamics, through action and conflict. Differences are not active; they have no internal source of change, thus change ends up being exogenous, untheorized, and, ultimately, incoherent.

## THE MAJOR THEORETICAL PARADIGMS

The history of work on masculinity largely mirrors the history of the dominant paradigmatic debates of social science, particularly sociology. The work has traveled from structural functionalism to Marxism and social psychology to more sophisticated synthetic approaches. New work can begin to analyze culture, history, power, and inequality while still deeply exploring emotional dynamics, identity, and small-scale interaction. Correspondingly, the project of the study of masculinity is not only an analytical study of the cultural dynamics of identity, ideology, and power but also a political and emotional project, an examination of and immersion into the exploration of new forms of political culture, gender relations, and personal identity.

The three main paradigms in work on masculinity have risen (and fallen) through a roughly sequential history, proceeding from the psychological/Freudian approach to the sex role/functionalist approach and now to the new social science approaches. It is time to move beyond early psychological and functionalist approaches while integrating some of their insights in new ways. The ultimate challenge is to identify the strengths of current and past approaches and continue to innovate conceptually, offering still deeper ways to study the phenomena of gender as a manifestation of the larger culture and society.

### The Psychological/Freudian Paradigm

Psychoanalytic approaches to studying masculinity and gender have had only limited success. They have often been hampered by essentialism and biological materialism, often failing to understand gender as a socially constructed entity that is the product of historical change. These approaches have also been limited by an overly individualistic approach that is unable to handle the macro level of culture and power. Still, the psychoanalytic approach, particularly in its more recent forms, has had success in understanding the psychology of male identity and in seeing masculinity as an internally complex and contradictory psychological system.

Freud's work at the turn of the twentieth century made significant steps toward the development of a social scientific study of masculinity (though that was certainly not Freud's explicit intention). Unfortunately he never concentrated in a sustained way on masculinity in its own right, and his work is saturated with biological determinism and traditional gender ideology. Nonetheless, he was able to open up in certain ways the apparently obvious, natural category that was masculinity. He was able to partially break from intellectual orthodoxy and question the foundations of European gender ideology.[1]

Ultimately orthodox psychoanalysis is a very limited approach, but Freud presents a number of guiding concepts that can be usefully synthesized with other approaches in developing new perspectives on masculinity. One is the deeply emotional nature of identity of any form, involving both conscious and unconscious dynamics. Another is the dynamic image of masculinity, which he never sees in a pure state. Indeed, Freud's work can be borrowed from and reinterpreted to help explore ways in which every individual personality is complex, changing over time, and internally contradictory at any one time. Approaches taking direction from Freud have been able to see the multifaceted nature of gendered identity, the ways in which heterosexuality and homosexuality are interwoven, and ways in which forms of femininities are always part of men's characters.[2]

Carl Jung's work represents another major psychoanalytic approach to the study of masculinities, one that is central to the work of a number of popular writers today, notably Robert Bly, one of the central guiding figures of the mythopoetic men's movement. Gender was an important focus of Jung's work, but ultimately his analysis fell into overly schematic and wildly speculative work on archetypes. Jung cast aside Freud's project of getting beyond the calcified male/female dichotomy through early notions of social constructionism and the concept of the fractured and contradictory nature of gender identity. Jung embraced instead the idea of gender as based in ahistorical archetypes, structures of the psyche that are immune to social effects both in one's life course and in the course of history itself.[3]

Later work on masculinity taking direction from Jung is even more misleading in many ways. An excellent example is one of the foundational texts of the mythopoetic movement, Robert Bly's *Iron John* (1990). While *Iron John* no doubt has had significant effects on the self-development of individual men, it is not useful from a social scientific point of view in developing new theories of masculinity. Bly digs his archetypes out of a folktale told by the Brothers Grimm, and he uses these archetypes independent of any developed sociocultural analysis that roots and traces these myths through social history. He then combines this material with other non-Western mythology in ways that are purely speculative and nonsystematic. Although this kind of approach can be useful, perhaps, as a metaphorical exploration, that is not Bly's intention. He takes the myths completely out of context, without historical ties to the modern era in any way, and considers them to be transcendent structures constituting every man across every historical period. Certainly Bly's work has had a major impact on the men's movement, but it is deeply, conceptually problematic as social scientific analysis.[4]

Psychoanalysis has been taken in more useful directions vis-à-vis masculinity work in the form of radical psychoanalysis, under the creative influences of Marxism and feminism. Marxist psychoanalysis made some strides with the work of Wilhelm Reich and the Frankfurt School. Although masculinity was never the explicit, overriding focus, some contributions were made through indirect exploration of the issues.[5] For instance, work by Theodor Adorno, Erich Fromm, and Max Horkheimer on authoritarian character types can be seen as studies of different forms of masculinity (Horkheimer 1936; Fromm 1942; Adorno et al. 1950).

While Marxist reinterpretations of psychoanalysis raised the potential of the psychoanalytic tradition, feminist work focused more specifically on gender, in part using insights from literary theory. Jacques Lacan was a key influence for European feminists such as Luce Irigaray and Juliet Mitchell. Psychoanalytic feminists take from Lacan the key conceptual development of shifting the physical focus of Freudian theory to a more sophisticated symbolic realm. Thus masculinity and the phallus become more fully constitutive elements in the culture of patriarchy. This further extension of Freud allows later psychoanalytic thinkers to work on constructing a more fully cultural theory. In this paradigm, the analysis of masculinity must be about complex relationships of symbols, of values that are part of the constitution of difference and power. For instance, it becomes possible to explore the range and variation in individual men's appropriation or lack thereof of the tools of masculine power. Men's relationships to certain forms of masculinity can be fully understood as a changing dynamic, one that is part of a fluid and contradictory sociocultural framework.[6]

American feminist psychoanalysis took a significantly more "down-to-earth" approach, centering more concretely on family relationships and early child development. Two of the main figures,

Nancy Chodorow (1978, 1985) and Dorothy Dinnerstein (1976), have worked on the issue of male gender development, appropriating Freud to examine identity formation through gendered relations with parents (see Gilligan [1982] for related work). While these are useful psychological tools for the analysis of male gender socialization, they are limited in focus and would only find their full utility in larger systemic theories of masculinities.

Overall, psychoanalytic approaches are of limited usefulness for the development of a full study of masculinity. They often fail to make the micro-macro link, content to stay on the psychological level, missing macrolevel issues of culture and power. Masculinity cannot be seen fully as a structured discourse in cultural terms. Further, psychoanalytic approaches are often essentialist in one way or another, making them unable to see gender as socially constructed and thus failing to see masculinity as a product of social change. Nonetheless, their insights can be incorporated into the larger study of masculinity, particularly through their contributions in the areas of understanding the psychology of male identity and in seeing masculinity as an internally complex and contradictory psychological system with fundamental roots in childhood development.

## The Sex Role/Functionalist Paradigm

Another major strand in masculinity research is the "sex role" framework that began in the 1940s and emerged directly from Émile Durkheim's work. Grounded in functionalism, the sex role approach shows a weakness in its inability to fully analyze power and inequality. Further, this approach generally has a rigid vision of action and identity, given its often overly deterministic, "top down," structuralist character. Correspondingly, social change is not fully theorized and, when dealt with, is often in contradiction with other aspects of the theory. In general, the early forms of this paradigm have been transcended in most current work on masculinity, but some of its key strengths have been incorporated into contemporary cultural approaches.

Functionalist sex role theory was the established, accepted approach to the study of gender in sociology by the 1950s. The use of the "role" concept goes back at least as far as the 1930s, but it was in the 1940s that Talcott Parsons first applied it to gender. Not surprisingly, there is little treatment in this paradigm of gender relations as involving power. Further, the argument is weakened by examining issues of sex and gender almost entirely from the context of the family (Parsons 1964a, 1964b). (Note that functionalists' use of the term *sex roles* predates the later acceptance of the sex/gender distinction. *Sex roles* is used in this book solely to refer to the functionalist term.)

Parsons's central approach in his later, more developed work was one integrating functionalism and the form of psychoanalysis popular at the time. His achievement was impressive in synthesizing a number of approaches and issues, namely microsensitive issues of patterned interaction in the family, the sexual division of labor, a structural approach to kinship, personality formation dynamics from psychoanalysis, and the socialization framework (Parsons and Bales 1956). His work established the fundamental focus on the differentiation and internalization of gender roles, still a popular thesis today. Unfortunately, gender roles themselves remained a taken-for-granted fact, a kind of "black box" approach that must be transcended in contemporary work. The focus in Parsons's work was on the processes and the structures that brought about gender roles. His work is ultimately an overly structural approach, and it is fallible to the kind of "oversocialization" critique that applies to functionalist work in general (Wrong 1961; Garfinkel 1967).

Not surprisingly, much subsequent research in this vein was on social problems of mothers and fathers, including family dysfunctions such as divorce, problematic maternal practices, juvenile delinquency, and intrafamilial conflict. Social subordination was not of interest for these researchers, nor were they theoretically equipped to adequately analyze such dynamics. Examples include Komarovsky (1946, 1950), Riesman (1953), Hacker (1957), Hartley (1959), Sexton (1969), and Bednarik (1970).

The framework of sex role theory soon came under increasing attack and was eventually rejected for the most part. One of the main weaknesses of the approach from the perspective of the study of masculinities is that one norm of male identity is supposed to be recognizable and accepted. However, this abstracting of one "pure" norm results in the majority of actual men not quite fitting this vision. In this approach expectations of men are generally cast as universal and fixed, and variations are often seen as residual, as deviance and "failures" of socialization. Variation and conflict is sometimes discussed in the tradition, but in two contradictory ways, both based in the essentialist fallacy. One approach is to slightly complicate the Parsonian vision by saying that men are being pushed to add expressive characteristics to their established instrumental identities. However, instead of seeing these dynamics as the result of the historical-cultural forces that have produced dominant masculinity to begin with, changes are seen as a threat to "true" masculinity, as in Bednarik (1970) and Sexton (1969). Thus the current mainstream form of masculinity is normalized as the only form of masculinity. The approach cannot see forms of masculinity as the results of social action and historical change through dynamics of negotiation, conflict, and power. Ultimately gender identity becomes a nonsocial essence, rooted in biology and genetics (though rarely explicitly argued as such by the author).[7]

The other explanatory device used by sex role theorists is the concept of role conflict. Here individuals have a full range of experiences in their lives that result in a range of personalities embodying a wide variety of forms of masculinity. However, there is conflict when a cultural norm of masculinity is overly constricting, demanding undue compliance to one form of masculinity. Thus there is a vision of some kind of nonsocial, natural degree of variation of masculinity. In this liberal vision, men are seen as victims of a dominating culture that does not allow their "true" selves to come forth. Again, masculinity is seen as having an ahistorical, presocial, essential nature (even if varied) that then comes into conflict with the social. While more dynamic than the orthodox functionalist approach, sex role theory succumbs to similar weaknesses.[8]

Sex role theory cannot properly handle the issue of social change. While the issue itself is often simply ignored by sex role theory adherents, there are those who do try to explore social change, including Pleck (1976, 1981) and Brannon (1976). Ultimately, however, masculinity is conceived in static, biostructural terms in this approach. Change, when discussed, is seen as exogenous, as something that happens to sex roles. Sometimes this is in macro, materialist terms, such as when economic or technological shifts produce changes in the male sex role. Other times this is in essentialist, nonsocial terms, as when the true nature of masculinity is seen as needing more freedom to express itself in the face of an overly controlling culture. Either way, change cannot be understood in this paradigm as an internal, fully social dynamic occurring within gender identities/relations.

Ultimately, the sex role approach observes reality (whether correctly or not) and then abstracts a normative image. Those within this perspective then generally take this status quo for granted, largely locked within the mainstream ideological context of their time. When they do otherwise, they are forced to appeal to essentialist, nonsocial categories. Further, an inherent part of this static approach is the discussion of differences between men and women, not relations between them. Relations can change through their own internal dynamics, through action and conflict. Differences are not active; they have no internal source of change, thus change must be exogenous. Any focus on power and conflict is correspondingly limited. Power and conflict as causal forces cannot be fully analyzed within gender relations because these sex differences are themselves not the result of a sociocultural history of power and conflict. At the level of theoretical logic, the position is varyingly essentialist, deeply confused, or both: "sex roles" just exist as a fact of sex difference. They are not adequately theorized as having been formed through a contingent cultural-historical process.[9]

*The New Social Science Approaches*

It was the advent of second-wave feminism and broad new intellectual approaches inclusive of culture, interaction, power, and conflict that led to the development of a generation of new social science approaches to the study of masculinity. This new work is spread across the social sciences but concentrated in sociology, history, and anthropology. There is no definitive, agreed-upon paradigm in this area, but the strongest of this scholarship centers around a number of key foci: the differences among varying forms of masculinities; the complex, contradictory nature of masculinity; the social construction of gender in microinteractional as well as historical processes; and the importance of economic, institutional, and cultural structures relating to identity and power.

Some of these new approaches borrow from new directions in microsociology, such as ethnomethodology, by looking at the ways in which gender is not rigidly predetermined but instead negotiated in small-scale interaction. This offers key insights into ways to address several central issues, for example how gender ideology is constructed in interaction by men as emotionally motivated individuals. It also contributes to an understanding of what the processes of contestation are that are involved in the ongoing ideological construction of masculinity (in this case, mythopoetic masculinity). Microsensitive approaches help examine the contingencies in ideological "work," that is to say, how and why certain paths of negotiation are directed, extended, or cut off by different men at different times. It becomes possible to examine closely the dynamics of emotional motivation as men pursue certain discursive ends vis-à-vis masculine identity.

One successful example of this tradition includes Messner's (1992) study of professional athletes. Using detailed interview data, he is able to explore how power and gender are negotiated and constructed in the highly masculinized field of professional sports. Alan M. Klein (1993) has a similar achievement with his ethnography of the male bodybuilding gym world. Within this tradition, researchers often explore the ways in which different ideological positions come into conflict and compete for dominance (even if this language is not used as such). Thus Gruneau and Whitson (1993), in studying the field of Canadian ice hockey, examine the ways in which those in power in business and politics have been able to develop and encourage the highly masculinized and violent hockey culture. This work also tends to include a sensitivity to interactional contingency, both in terms of material and ideal dynamics. For instance, the studies mentioned earlier in this section examine the ways in which the ongoing process of gendered identity construction is affected by varying cultural and economic dynamics, by physical prowess or injuries, and by internal contradictions in the gender ideology of professional sports. All of these dynamics become situationally meaningful at varying times and places, and although they often operate unconsciously, they can also be utilized strategically by individuals toward certain ideological ends.

Analysis of the cultural qualities of institutional settings plays a key role in this work. This issue is central to the research presented in this book, given the focus on the cultural environment of the mythopoetic men's movement and how the men in it evaluate and change it according to their conceptions of what the movement should be achieving. In previous work addressing these issues, local cultures have been seen as tied to and growing out of the dynamics of the context of an organized institution. For instance, Messner and others (Messner 1992, 2000, 2002; Messner and Sabo 1990, 1994; McKay, Messner, and Sabo 2000) examine how the sports world is constituted in a hierarchical, competitive structure. The result is that young men who enter this world are being socialized into an institutional culture. Successful work in this tradition has also been done at the empirical site of the workplace (Collinson, Knights, and Collinson 1990; Donaldson 1991).

Willis's (1977) pioneering work can also be read today as a highly nuanced look at the social construction of ideologies of masculinity. While he explicitly focuses on class and reproduction, he makes key insights into issues of gender ideology. For instance, he not only looks at the differences between class or race settings vis-à-vis masculinity but also examines the dynamics involved in the emergence of differing and opposed masculinities within the same institutional setting. This is a key achievement that is quite instructive for the study of culture and ideology on an internal and local level.

The work I have just discussed goes a long way in examining the variety of masculinities as well as the conflict and negotiation that go on within and between them. However, a key advance that incorporates these insights and goes beyond them is the concept of hegemonic masculinity. This is integral to the current analysis given the interest in how the men of the mythopoetic movement conceptualize the restrictions and limitations that they feel have been imposed upon them through the dominant gender culture. The men's view of hegemonic masculinity steers their critical response to it in terms of constructing an alternative, mythopoetic masculinity. With these recent developments in masculinity work, research is able to analyze in a more developed manner the relationships between the different forms of masculinities and the power differences between them. The concept of hegemonic masculinity allows the study of the social construction of masculinities through ideologies and practices of social control, discrimination, and manipulation.[10]

The study of hegemonic masculinity, first defined by Carrigan, Connell, and Lee (1985), involves examining the dominant discourse of masculinity and how it restricts and suppresses alternative masculinities. The dominant form is generally seen as institutionalized in concrete social arrangements in which certain individuals, whose identities are constituted in the dominant cultural/psychological forms, are accorded power. Through pursuing and maintaining their internalized world view, individuals who live according to the dominant perspective are understood to be generally maintaining the status quo (though largely unconsciously), which tends to maintain certain benefits that they receive, namely unequal power and greater access to scarce resources. In this perspective, men and women alike can both benefit and suffer from the dynamics of hegemonic masculinity. Men, and in particular certain kinds of men, benefit disproportionately from hegemonic arrangements. However, it is possible for some women to have more of the culturally hegemonic characteristics than some men, and thus they can benefit accordingly. Further, men are seen as being judged through, and in explicit competition through, the evaluative framework of the dominant discourse of masculinity.

This perspective studies masculinity (and gender more broadly), but inasmuch as masculinity is part of the dominant culture of a society, the perspective also studies hegemony and cultural politics in general. As in other studies of hegemony, the culturally dominant features are seen as corresponding to a relatively small group of existing individuals. The result is that the vast majority of men do not possess the full set of hegemonic characteristics. This allows the analysis of the ideological and material inequality not only of women vis-à-vis gender but also of men. Among other things, it becomes possible to study the ways in which women and disempowered men can and do support hegemonic masculinity against their own "interests" (broadly defined). The dynamics of culture, power, and inequality are much more nuanced in this approach than in earlier models.

One of the strengths of hegemony models is that they can begin to more fully theorize change, contingency, and negotiation. They can avoid the overly macro, unidimensional, traditional oppression models in which those in power essentially have total control and/or those out of power are essentially totally dominated, with no path for liberational change. With mature hegemony approaches, resistance and opposition are more fully integrated and their potential success is a central part of the approach. In a fully cultural model, the meaning of any act or event can be negotiated and debated according to symbolic structures that are partially autonomous from power, with real consequences not only for empirical individuals but also for the very structure and meaning of the ideologies themselves.[11]

In these ways, hegemony models involve an appreciation of the dialectical nature of the relationships constructing masculinity. Causality is multilinear, transcending simple unicausal socialization and reproduction models. Hegemonic masculinity is generally advocated from above and, when it succeeds, helps reproduce the existing system. However, males can resist this power and use their own autonomy to create oppositional masculinities (see, for example, Willis 1977). Thus, the meaning of masculinity is a site of conflict between different groups of males, involving much more than a direct reproduction of the ideology of those in power. For example, Connell (1989) supports these findings both theoretically and empirically as well as showing more fully the ways in which masculine subcultures while competing among themselves can often still share exclusionary and oppressive characteristics.

Further insights in this developing body of work include the analysis of contradictions and tensions within symbolic systems. This creates a more nuanced understanding, allowing a detailed exploration, beyond mere description, of the internal dynamics of gender discourses. This is useful in the current study for looking at the tensions within mythopoetic masculinity as the men exhibit it. As I explore in detail in chapters 3 through 5, ideological contestation between group members is often the playing out of symbolic tensions contained within the discourse itself.

The strength of much of this literature is the ways in which it can analyze identities in general, and masculinities in particular, as ongoing processes, on both an individual level and a collective level. This avoids the static vision of types of masculinity as fixed categories that is too frequently the model for psychoanalytic work and a constant danger for any work on gender. In the older conceptualizations, change can only happen through individuals switching from one type to another, making a jump into a different category. However, this does not describe the actual dynamics in the complex processes of empirical reality. The same mistake is made on a more macro level, where there can be a shift from one dominant form of masculinity to another. What this lacks is an appreciation of the ways in which future aspects of masculinity are contained within present forms in a dialectical manner. Thus, change must be seen as a process, not as discrete transfers from one form to another.

In much of this more sophisticated recent work, men can be seen as consciously changing themselves while at the same time they can be seen as changing on a nonconscious level, as part of larger historical-cultural changes.[12] This is done through empirical analysis, in an historicist style of analysis. Thus men are analyzed vis-à-vis their own agency and conscious decision making while at the same time they are seen as part of larger cultural contexts and as part of larger historical processes. Certainly this varies in focus, but the fundamental commitment is an historicist, synthetic one.

An effective example of work with a sensitivity to issues of change and issues of contingency/agency is Cockburn's (1983) study of the collective construction of masculinity in London print shops. She explores the ways in which the print shop culture is changing due to internal individual initiative, external legal and social pressures, and the larger cultural changes that increasingly frame the traditional practices as outdated and unjust. On a micro level, these larger changes manifest themselves through more culturally progressive recruits to the print shop world, boys who have an ideological framework that is less patriarchal, less given to subservience, that is, in short, challenging to the old print shop cultural order. Corman et al. (1993) explore some of the same issues in examining the processes surrounding the increased inclusion of women in the Canadian steel industry. The work is a subtly nuanced analysis, incorporating individual agency, power, larger cultural change, and collective action.

Work in this vein is also beginning to emerge from the Marxist tradition. As part of the focus on masculinity, there is a useful critique of orthodox Marxist theory. Hearn offers sophisticated examples of this new approach, recasting Marxist analysis to examine men's labor in the context of a more cultural sense of patriarchy (Hearn 1987; Hearn and Morgan 1990; Hearn and Parkin 2001). While this work still retains some weaknesses of materialist/orthodox Marxist approaches (albeit in a milder form), it is a step in the right direction for a tradition that has tended to produce rather crude models of gender and gender identity. Others similarly innovating within the Marxist tradition include Brittan (1989), Segal (1990, 1999), and Seidler (1989, 1991). In a broad sense, cultural Marxist work in this vein effectively demonstrates the necessity of studying masculinity as an integral part of larger cultural and social structures and processes.[13]

## PREVIOUS APPROACHES TO STUDYING THE MYTHOPOETIC MEN'S MOVEMENT

Having discussed the study of masculinity in general, it is instructive to conclude with a brief review of some of the previous research examining the mythopoetic men's movement. Most scholarship on the topic has focused on the writings of the popular authors who helped inspire the movement, such as Robert Bly, Douglas Gillette, James Hillman, Sam Keen, Michael Meade, and Robert Moore. The focus tends to be on examining these texts' weaknesses, of which there are many. Some of the exemplary work in this category includes that by Clatterbaugh (1997), Connell (1995, 2005), Ferber (2000), Kimmel and Kaufman (1994), Messner (1997), and Newton (2005). These works very effectively expose books such as Robert Bly's *Iron John* (1990) and Sam Keen's *Fire in the Belly* (1991) for their many shortcomings. These movement books are full of shoddy scholarship, including erroneous manipulation of mythology and non-Western cultural ideas. They contain many ungrounded statements about gender as well as inaccurate historical assertions, and they contain numerous essentialist points about gender, repeatedly making appeals to an essential masculinity, or a "deep masculinity" that is ahistorical and unshaped by culture. Further, the texts are accurately criticized as, at points, having some conservative and somewhat antifeminist political and cultural ideas. Certainly texts of the mythopoetic men's movement are not clarion calls to progressive political activism; their emphasis is much more on personal, therapeutic change.

It is important to understand the content of these movement texts inasmuch as they inspire the movement and obviously have effects on what movement participants think and do. However, the shortcoming of most previous scholarship on the topic is that it stops at the analysis of movement writings, not delving deeper into the movement itself with sustained empirical analysis of the participants themselves. This would require interviews, participant observation, or surveys to directly study what these men think and do. This data cannot be gathered from the writings of leaders. As a result, this set of analyses is incomplete, providing excellent background on the inspirational texts of the movement but not studying what the movement is actually doing.[14]

A good example of this approach is the piece titled "Weekend Warriors: The New Men's Movement," by Michael Kimmel and Michael Kaufman (1994), two of the leading scholars in the field of men's studies. Their analysis starts with this pejorative title and then criticizes the movement as being nonfeminist and essentialist as well as misguided in its psychoanalytic, anthropological, and historical assertions. I fully concur with these findings concerning the writings of movement writers, but their research cannot determine the extent to which these findings also hold for the movement as a whole, because it does not empirically study the movement itself. The almost sole source of data for Kimmel and Kaufman is the text of Bly's *Iron John* (1990). The rest of the chapter is made up of discussion and citations of other writers who themselves have done almost no empirical research on the movement. One of the only citations of direct evidence is secondary and journalistic, not social scientific (Chapple and Talbot 1990). Further, even this citation is primarily about Robert Bly rather than about grassroots participants.

Kimmel repeats this critique of the men's movement in his excellent book *Manhood in America* (1996). Others generate similar results with similar methods (e.g., Clatterbaugh 1997; Connell 1995, 2005; Ferber 2000; Newton 2005). Again the focus is almost entirely on the written works of Bly and other movement leaders, with occasional secondary analysis. At times the authors of these works about the movement comment on weekend retreats or workshops, but they are casual references without systematic data gathering. Further, the retreats and workshops are the sites of the movement that are the most extreme and easiest to caricature. These authors ignore weekly small-group discussion meetings, which are significantly more complex ideologically and less leader-driven. They are also (probably not coincidently) more challenging and time-consuming to study. Adding to all of this, the authors cite each other repeatedly, creating a kind of circular "echo effect," where repetition serves to cement the ideas.

The small number of works that do study the movement directly provides some of the missing analysis and paints a more complex picture of the movement (e.g., Barton 2000; Schwalbe 1995, 1996). The most successful of this work is Schwalbe's 1996 book, *Unlocking the Iron Cage: The Men's Movement, Gender Politics, and American Culture.* In this ethnography, Schwalbe confirms earlier suspicions that the men's movement is not a resolutely feminist movement, that it has some conservative elements, and that it contains some essentialist thinking about gender. Interestingly, however, his data suggest what he calls "loose essentialism" as opposed to the full essentialism of which Bly and others are sometimes accused.[15] The data in my research indicate a similar finding: at times the men draw on essentialist ideas from the movement texts, but at other times they reject essentialism. It is a casual, weak, and intermittent essentialism that has no deep belief behind it. As a general practice, in the moment of creative interaction in the groups, written texts are only rarely mentioned or drawn upon and when they are it is sometimes to disagree with them. In fact, with reference to essentialism specifically, a foundational goal of the movement is to change the gender identity of individual men, completely contrary to the essentialist belief that gender identity is fixed and timeless.

It is interesting to note that Messner (1997), writing after Schwalbe, has a significantly more nuanced understanding than many authors who either wrote before Schwalbe or do not cite his work. Although Messner also does not conduct empirical research on movement participants, he cites Schwalbe repeatedly in developing and supporting his analysis. He notes that "*At least on its surface,* this mythopoetic discourse appears to be part of a contemporary anti-feminist backlash" (1997, 20; italics added). He then cites Schwalbe's research to suggest that the situation is more complicated than this, that in fact the mythopoetic men are apolitical, focusing on personal change and spiritual goals. Certainly a movement that matches this description can only be seen as conservative if *conservative* is defined as anything that is not clearly liberal or progressive. This is erroneous, because it ignores the possibility that a movement can be internally mixed politically and on average simply moderate or mildly liberal without being either conservative or strongly progressive. In fact, in his complex categorization scheme, Messner carefully separates the mythopoetic movement from the clearly antifeminist and conservative Promise Keepers and men's rights movements. This is unlike some casual analysts who lump all three together without close empirical study.

The empirical analysis in chapters 4 and 5 will bring out these issues further. However, at this point, it is important to acknowledge that the mythopoetic movement is certainly not a major champion of feminist ideals and progressive politics. It largely ignores issues of inequality, whether they are related to gender, race, or class. It is not focused on changing the political, legal, or economic systems, and it is composed mostly of white, heterosexual men from the middle and upper classes. However, examined closely, none of these characteristics makes the mythopoetic men's movement a necessarily conservative phenomenon. In fact, in chapters 4 and 5 I show that it is a moderately liberal movement devoted to doing many of the things that feminists have been calling on men to do for decades, namely to become more emotionally developed so that they are better fathers and partners and generally more devoted to family and community instead of to their own personal freedom, prestige, and economic accumulation. Thus the goal of the men's movement is not political change as it is traditionally conceived but, rather, psychological and cultural change. From the political standpoint of progressive politics and feminism, the movement can certainly be seen as flawed in many ways, but it is important to understand its unusual strengths as well.

Feminist scholars are not univocal on this point. In fact, some have pointed out that the movement makes some positive contributions from a feminist perspective. Writing in the journal *Feminist Issues*, Diane Richard-Allerdyce (1994) argues that the movement is helping men find their voices of alternative consciousness, separate and apart from traditional, dominant modes of masculinity. She points out that if women expect men to participate more fully in child care, these men had better shift their ways of thinking or they will simply pass on to their children the same cultural beliefs that they received as boys. Understanding socialization and cultural transmission in these ways makes it obvious that psychological change on the part of men is of central importance to the feminist project. She points out that social change involves more than public activism and that psychological change is an important component. Certainly the history of feminist consciousness-raising groups shows this. In fact, the early roots of the mythopoetic movement go back to the 1970s, when progressive men started developing discussion groups based directly on women's consciousness-raising groups. Eisler (1992), writing in *Women Respond to the Men's Movement: A Feminist Collection* (Hagan 1992), points out similar overlaps between the psychological and cultural elements of the feminist women's movement and the mythopoetic men's movement. In fact, the mythopoetic men's movement can be seen as a transitional movement, internally contradictory, carrying both hegemonic and counterhegemonic beliefs. With its more progressive elements, it is contributing some new, constructive ideas in the middle of the larger historical process of gender transformation. While the men's movement is bogged down with significant aspects of traditional ideology, it also challenges men in some progressive ways to change the way they think about themselves and to change the ways they participate in families and society at large.

Gloria Steinem (1992) writes, "Make no mistake about it: Women want a men's movement. We are literally dying for it. If you doubt that, just listen to women's desperate testimonies of hope that the men in our lives will become more nurturing toward children, more able to talk about emotions, less hooked on a spectrum of control that extends from not listening enough through to violence, and less repressive of their own human qualities that are called 'feminine'—and thus suppressed by cultures in which men dominate" (1992, v). Although Steinem is justly critical of the movement at other points in her piece, I believe that the succeeding chapters in this book will show that the participants are making changes that positively address each of her points that I have just quoted in one way or another.

I have chosen not to devote a lot of space to the writings of mythopoetic leaders because, as I have discussed, I generally agree with the already extensive, excellent critical work on the topic produced by others. Indeed, the particular contribution of my book is to fill in the gaps left by this body of work due to its methodological limitations and to simultaneously complement and add to the small amount of previous scholarship that uses interviewing and participant observation. This book, with its unique contribution to the synthesis of cultural sociology, the study of power, and the method of ethnography, offers a new and complex understanding of this most unusual phenomenon, the mythopoetic men's movement.

## CONCLUSION

The study of masculinity lies at a crossroads. The time has come to finally reject older perspectives such as orthodox psychological and, specifically, psychoanalytic approaches. Further, the sex role/functionalist paradigm must be rejected in favor of new cultural approaches. The new social science of masculinity is beginning to take a number of powerful, innovative directions, opening doors for the further growth of this promising field. The work is interdisciplinary and is developing from many different theoretical traditions. The new synthetic approaches exhibit the coming together of feminism, cultural sociology, history, cultural anthropology, race and ethnicity studies, Marxism, psychoanalysis, and gay and lesbian studies. They draw on a wide range of methodological traditions, including participant observation, interviewing, comparative/historical methods, and survey research, among others. Traditional debates and central, limiting dichotomies are being challenged, including the micro-macro divide, the structure-agency debate, and the materialist-idealist dichotomy. Further, traditional divisions between research methodologies are being bridged. Pursuing these strengths and avoiding previous errors can make it possible to further develop the study of gender, culture, power, identity, interactional dynamics, and many other foci. It is into this history that this book steps. Specifically, the analysis in chapters

3–6 will draw on the insights discussed here regarding hegemonic masculinity, culture structures, contingency and interaction, social constructionism, power, and social change. Innovating within the contemporary tradition of cultural sociology using ethnographic methods, the current study aims to synthesize many of the most recent strengths within masculinity studies while at the same time taking a new step into the study of culture and discourse.

## NOTES

1. For a very early feminist psychoanalysis drawing out these concepts from Freud, see Karen Horney (1932). For further discussion concerning these issues in the psychoanalytic tradition, see Chodorow (1978) and Garrison (1981). Other related early pieces on masculinity include Boehm (1930) and M. Klein (1928).

2. Unfortunately, the period following this exploratory time for psychoanalysis marked a decided turn away from some of this initial promise. This development appropriately earned psychoanalysis criticism as a rigid, biologically centered, conservative, and normalizing framework. Psychoanalysis became a conservative force that reflected popular cultural beliefs of the time.

3. This search took Jung to a presumed "beginning of history" to find the ultimate structure of human identity. He scoured world religions and ancient arts, and his later work separated almost entirely from clinical, empirical work and become a hopelessly speculative enterprise, jettisoning the previous gains of psychoanalysis. Rather than use this ancient religious material as metaphors or clues to current analysis, he took them as transcendent truths, outside the processes of social change. Jung's approach fails in this regard, as does biological materialism/essentialism.

4. For a provocative discussion of these issues, see Connell (1995).

5. Reich was interested in a micro-macro synthetic approach to ideology and identity. A key insight was the analysis of the "authoritarian family" as the means for the reproduction of class hierarchy and patriarchy (Reich 1970, 1972). This theoretical development of connecting larger social structural issues with identity took Freud to the next logical sociological step. Regrettably, Reich never pursued the examination of masculinity itself as a central dynamic in these social processes.

6. For more on the development of Lacanian psychoanalysis, see Roudinesco (1990). To explore further its explicitly feminist forms, see Grosz (1990), Irigaray (1985), and Mitchell (1975).

7. See Carrigan, Connell, and Lee (1985) for a further discussion of these important issues.

8. For a thoughtful analysis of the internal incoherence of the general role framework itself, see Connell (1979).

9. For further theoretical critique of the sex role paradigm, see Carrigan, Connell, and Lee (1985), Stacey and Thorne (1985), Kimmel (1987), and Connell (1995).

10. See Connell (2005) for an insightful analysis of this body of research.

11. An example is Messner's work on sports and sporting culture, where male violence is generally celebrated (Messner 1992; Messner and Sabo 1990). Detailed interactional analysis shows that the hegemonic cultural system is being constantly interpreted and sometimes altered.

12. Along these lines, this body of work represents a (mostly untheorized) contribution to the ongoing project of the further synthesizing of the agency/structure dichotomy.

13. For more on the history of masculinity scholarship, see Connell (1995). He analyzes, among other things, anthropological work done in the area of non-Western masculinity, a topic beyond the scope of the current discussion.

14. Bartkowski (2000, 2002, 2003) shows the ways in which incomplete understandings of men's movement beliefs and actions are a logical result when scholars focus only on the writings of elite leaders.

15. See Karides (1998) for a more detailed discussion of the strengths of Schwalbe's (1996) research.

# 3

# The Power of the
# Organic Intellectual

This chapter explores the complex dynamics of small-group inter-action, ideological construction, and consciousness-raising in the mythopoetic men's movement through a close empirical analysis of the role of the individual men's group leader. A major theoretical foundation of this exploration is Antonio Gramsci's work on ideol-ogy, social change, and the organic intellectual. Detailed ethnographic analysis shows that the leader is able to utilize his authority and interactional power to develop the ideological identity of the group and act as a socializing agent to its members. He can be understood as a Gramscian organic intellectual, disseminating and interpreting the ideas of the high intellectuals of the men's movement in order to develop the metaphorical foot soldiers who are the grassroots heart of the movement. At times this microlevel power is used to manipulate and control participants in the name of the local leader's ideological vision. The case study analysis that follows examines in empirical depth the complex interactional dynamics involving Watani, the "facilitator/firetender" of the Open Plain Men's Circle.

In the following analysis, the precise micropractices of Watani are explored in detail, exposing his role as organic intellectual as he ideologically directs the movement members. The data suggest a set of seven core practices that he invokes as a means toward the political socialization of the men in his organization. He is able to define, disseminate, and maintain a certain specific set of ideas and standards through his arsenal of micropractices of interactional power. This is a very conscious and strategic effort to maintain high levels

43

of focused commitment, participation, and psychological change, all moving in the leader's desired direction. He is trying to develop a cadre of highly motivated movement participants who will work toward the creation of his version of counterhegemonic masculinity and correspondingly transformed social consciousness. At the same time, his power is far from total, and group interaction is also a site for contestation and negotiation, with individual members challenging Watani's authority and discussing alternative conceptualizations. Interpretative outcomes cannot be perfectly predicted because they are open to the contingencies of individual initiative and the ongoing negotiation of meaning.

## CONSCIOUSNESS-RAISING AND SOCIAL CHANGE

Consciousness-raising is a major part of contemporary social movements and, when broadly defined, has been a part of social movements throughout history. Still, the process itself remains underexplored in social scientific research. While it has been studied extensively within the subfield of small-group research, it is still underappreciated within the study of social movements and social change more broadly. This is not surprising for Marxist work, which has, over its history, had a tendency to reduce the cultural component of social action to the material component, as discussed in chapter 2. Additionally, macro-oriented work of all kinds has tended to underappreciate the extent to which the very nature and historical path of social movements is constructed through interaction between subjective, motivated individuals. I pursue a voluntaristic and cultural approach that recovers agency as a crucial component of understanding the mythopoetic movement (as well as other social movements).

When studied at all, consciousness-raising is sometimes treated as if it were solely subjective and personal, unrelated to and unconcerned with larger social dynamics. It is often seen as a practice that has outlived itself, a practice whose importance is limited to the historical study of social movements. Instead, consciousness-raising must be understood as an ever-present component of all social movements, past, present, and future. Indeed, it is precisely this personal and political process that creates the necessary link between identity and historical experience. In this way people come together to understand what is shared across a broad category (or class) of people. The success of any social movement depends on this construction: seeing that one's own very personal, local experience is indeed a *social* phenomenon, a common experience with a common cause. If individuals are convinced that this common cause can be changed, then what is commonly referred to as a social movement can fully arise (Seidler 1991). This process of ideological construction and negotiation is a complex one, a process of contingent action and a cultural achievement with its own internal logic.

Another misunderstanding often made with respect to consciousness-raising is that it is a stage through which individuals must go *prior* to becoming political. However, this merely reproduces the larger conceptual split between public and private, a philosophical framework that permeates Western culture. Following this flawed perspective, an act is often understood as not being truly political until it occurs in the macropublic realm. Thus, if consciousness-raising deals with one's own private, individual experience, it becomes the predecessor to serious political engagement. Thus it can be seen as merely a remedial activity for the politically naive.

These misunderstandings vis-à-vis the issues surrounding consciousness-raising have been exposed and effectively countered by feminist and/or social movement scholars for decades (e.g., Hall and Jacques 1989; Hall and Jefferson 1989; Jacoby 1975; Rowbotham 1981, 1989; Segal 1990; Seidler 1986, 1991). Still, they persist implicitly, and often explicitly, in social scientific treatment of social movements. Often the prejudices against consciousness-raising do not show up in a researcher's work directly; they show up instead in absence, in the relative lack of serious attention paid to consciousness-raising in the first place (Seidler 1991). In the study of the mythopoetic men's movement, it becomes obvious that understanding the intricacies involved in the process of consciousness-raising is central to understanding the nature of the movement itself.

## GRAMSCI AND THE ORGANIC INTELLECTUAL

It is the appreciation of the importance of consciousness-raising in the study of social movements that serves as the foundation for exploring the process of constructing and negotiating a counterhegemonic ideology on the part of the men in the mythopoetic movement. The seminal work of Antonio Gramsci on ideology and social change is the central jumping off point for this analysis. He argues that social change necessitates the dissemination and internalization of new modes of thinking and new ideologies. "Creating a new culture does not only mean one's own individual 'original' discoveries. It also, and most particularly, means the diffusion in a critical form of truths already discovered, their 'socialization' as it were, and even making them the basis of vital action, an element of coordination and intellectual and moral order" (Gramsci 1971, 328). This important insight opens the door to the detailed study of the cultural dynamics of consciousness-raising.

Gramscian theories of ideology can be productively applied to the role of the leader of mythopoetic men's groups. Watani, as the key socializing agent of the Open Plain Men's Circle, can be understood as disseminating a new vision of the world within his men's groups and through broader movement events. The concept of the organic intellectual, a central component of Gramsci's theory, proves useful in understanding these empirical dynamics.

As Gramsci's work explores, the organic intellectual is the necessary link between the high intellectuals and the population at large, the one who brings progressive and potentially liberating new moral visions to the attention of the people. S/he is a teacher and a guide, a leader who helps others construct a sense of some injustice under which they live. S/he is a conduit for a new way of thinking that casts an original, critical light on circumstances that expose what can be seen as the inequality and suffering that had been hitherto taken for granted and accepted as the natural order of things. It is this leadership, by both elite intellectuals and organic intellectuals, that is central to the dynamics of social change. As Gramsci argues, "A human mass does not 'distinguish' itself, does not become independent in its own right without, in the widest sense, organizing itself; and there is no organization without intellectuals, that is, without organizers and leaders, in other words, without the theoretical aspect of the theory-practice nexus being distinguished concretely by the existence of a group of people 'specialized' in conceptual and philosophical elaboration of ideas" (Gramsci 1971, 335).

This conceptual model is useful for more fully understanding the mythopoetic men's movement. While the first embryonic glimmerings of the movement preceded the writings of the core high intellectuals of the movement, it was not until the publication and broad consumption of these writings that the movement really took off. It is the popular work of movement intellectuals such as Robert Bly, James Hillman, Sam Keen, and Michael Meade (e.g., Bly 1990; Bly, Hillman, and Meade 1992; Hillman 1989; Keen 1989, 1991; Mahdi, Christopher, and Meade 1996; and Meade 1993) that provided the ideological direction posts for the formation and continuation of a grassroots movement. They articulate many of the ideas that inspire the movement.

It is the work of lower-level movement activists to interpret this work, further its consumption, and apply it in an immediate way to actual men's lives and to organize men in groups that constitute the institutionalization of the movement. They are the organic intellectuals without which there would be no movement. Without them, the result would be individual men, only vaguely aware of each others' existence, reading books and interpreting them on their own. There would be no unified conception of the ideology of these texts and, most importantly, there would be no groups, no organizations, and no movement. Watani is one of this handful of local organic intellectuals who together create a web of organizers that loosely unifies the members across the country into a national movement.[1]

One of the crucial jobs that Watani does as an organic intellectual is to help give a voice to the partially formed feelings of frustration, unease, and dissatisfaction that dwell within the men in the group. As Gramsci and many others argue, it is clear that prior to the coalescence of any social movement, the future members of that movement have unresolved feelings of discontent that are only partially theorized and not well organized into a shared sense of common cause. It is a situation of ideological contradiction (Gramsci 1971, 333). Individuals feel an amorphous sense of dissatisfaction; they have a vague consciousness of something being wrong, but they have currently available to them only a set of cultural ideologies that does not satisfactorily explain these feelings. It is a liminal cultural moment; the potential is high for an instigating development that may well have enormous effect. It is at this point that a social movement can be triggered if a hegemonic ideology can be identified and a counterhegemonic vision can be articulated and spread among the disaffected. Gramsci states,

> Critical understanding of self takes place therefore through a struggle of political "hegemonies" and of opposing directions . . . in order to arrive at the working out at a higher level of one's own conception of reality. [This is] . . . a part of the historical process, whose elementary and primitive phase is to be found in the sense of being "different" and "apart," in an instinctive feeling of independence, and which progresses to the level of real possession of a single and coherent conception of the world. (1971, 334)

In fact, the formation of a sense of hegemony itself is a major step in the development of a social movement: "This is why it must be stressed that the political development of the concept of hegemony represents a great philosophical advance as well as a politico-practical one. For it necessarily supposes an intellectual unity and an ethic in conformity with a conception of reality that has gone beyond common sense and has become, if only within narrow limits, a critical conception" (Gramsci 1971, 334). In many ways, this becomes the job of the individual men's group leader. I explore this in more detail later in this chapter using detailed ethnographic data.

## LEADERSHIP, POWER, CONTROL, AND SOCIALIZATION

Watani is constantly at work monitoring the men's group and using many different microresources to shape the ideological and behavioral developments within the group and within the members' larger lives. The prevalent qualities of the men's group are constantly negotiated in situated interaction, a process of interaction over which Watani attempts to exercise significant control. He sees it as his right and duty to keep the group following what he defines as the important principles of the movement. He sees himself as working to make changes in society, one man at a time. Putting it in the strongest sense, he considers himself to be on a personal and spiritual mission to help save society from what he sees as the negative effects of hegemonic masculinity and other related beliefs and practices.

It is from this base of motivation that Watani's role can be better understood through the concept of the organic intellectual. On the micro level, a significant portion of Watani's life is devoted to steering men in a certain direction, encouraging them to recognize the concept of hegemonic masculinity and appreciate certain alternatives. He does this through very practical, microlevel mechanisms of socialization, which constitute the process of consciousness-raising and of social control on the interactional level. In this role, he uses his power to encourage, motivate, and, at times, manipulate group members.

Watani does strategic work to bring about certain desired outcomes. He is far from completely successful at reaching the goal of "perfect" socialization; his attempts are sometimes contested and thwarted by members of the group, and he contradicts himself sometimes. Further, an interpretation of a particular event during a meeting or outside of the group context is often indeterminate in terms of its meaning; it is open to symbolic negotiation and Watani cannot be sure how it will be understood. In the end, group beliefs and actions are a continuous achievement, debated, fought over, violated, reconstituted, and negotiated.

## UNDERSTANDING GROUP PROCESSES OF SOCIALIZATION

Previous social psychological work on group processes related to socialization and microlevel control is helpful in further understanding the mythopoetic men's movement in this respect. One useful concept developed in this area is that of a cohesive group, that is, one whose members generally stick together and remain unified in pursuit of group goals (Carron 1982; Mudrack 1989). Cohesive groups are typified by strong ties between members and the general phenomenon of members perceiving events in similar terms (Braaten 1991; Evans and Jarvis 1980). As I discuss later in this chapter, men's groups can be understood in these terms; they have an explicit commitment to the ideal of consensus and group unity. The men in the groups are expected to know each other well, think in similar ways, and support each other.

The leader has a complex role in this cohesive context. The dynamic accords the leader a certain amount of power, given that disagreement and discord is generally kept to a minimum. At the same time, he is also limited in his power to unilaterally impose unpopular rules and interpretations because the men have strong ties to each other and look out for each other's interests. If the participants sense that something the leader does is unjust, the men can make strong claims on their own collective behalf. Given these factors, the leader must carefully negotiate his interactions within this field of cohesive group dynamics.

Work on group judgment and categorization is also helpful for further understanding the processes of socialization and social control within the mythopoetic men's movement. Small groups are continuously engaged in appraising or assessing the attributes of an object of focus. Groups working together on some common goal must make collective judgments and resolve conflicts that arise when members hold different conceptions of reality (Asch 1956; Brehmer 1976; Hastie 1986). One way in which a leader can help direct group conceptualizations in this context is through what has been called promotional leadership (Janis 1982). Here the leader strongly advocates certain positions and opposes others. While this practice cannot be used in an overbearing way in men's groups, the data in this chapter show that it is a method that is productively drawn upon by Watani in trying to steer group evaluations and mediate between members' differing interpretations of actions and individuals.

Promotional leadership is effective at discouraging dissent and creating strong feelings of in-group morality, as previous empirical research has suggested (Fodor and Smith 1982; Leana 1985; Moorhead and Montanari 1986).[2] The men's group context is one devoted to the learning of techniques of evaluation and to the application of these techniques in very detailed ways to the lives of individual members. The leader is not interested in the techniques themselves being debated. The group discussion is meant to focus primarily on the use of these conceptual tools, not their creation or development. Thus, promotional leadership, while it is sometimes contested, generally succeeds at promoting political socialization vis-à-vis central movement ideals.

The concept of coercive tactics is another analytical tool that is productive in further understanding the socialization practices of the men's group leader as organic intellectual. Coercive tactics are threats and actual damage delivered by someone in a group who has a certain amount of power based on his or her position in some social structure (Lawler 1992). Threats signal the intention of doing harm of some sort and explicitly warn an individual of a negative consequence to certain kinds of action (Deutsch 1973; Tedeschi, Schlenker, and Bonoma 1973). Threats do not have to be explicit, nor do they have to be verbalized in order to be effective (Schelling 1960).[3]

The analysis in this chapter shows the effective use of coercive tactics on Watani's part. He is constituted as the leader of the group and as a source of knowledge because of his position in the larger social movement. Watani is accorded power by the members because of their culturally constituted beliefs about him. Due to this dynamic, he has the power to use coercive tactics, which he does on occasion. Because of other conflicting local norms, he cannot use these tactics frequently, but when he does use them they are generally effective. The data later in this chapter show this particularly in the case of his selection of new members, the sanctioning of moral and behavioral breaches, and his removal of group members.

To be sure, social psychological work in this area is limited by its lack of appreciation of cultural issues and its frequent inability to deal effectively with power. Nonetheless, it offers a number of useful conceptual tools to help understand the microdynamics of socialization and consciousness-raising in the mythopoetic group context. Specifically, men's groups are cohesive groups that aim to create group unity, develop strong intragroup ties, and encourage similar thinking between members. This foundational definition of the group generally empowers the leader in his goals of political socialization. At times, however, group unity can help in resistance to a leader's efforts if they are collectively opposed. Given these conceptual tools, it becomes possible to examine on a closer level the precise practices of socialization and control that Watani utilizes in his role as organic intellectual of the mythopoetic men's movement.

## FURTHER DESCRIPTION OF THE MYTHOPOETIC MEN'S GROUP

Before proceeding, it would be useful to describe further the men's group meeting format. The general basis of the meeting is premised on the Native American council style approach, that is, a ritualistic coming together of community members to share feelings and beliefs and to make decisions as a close-knit group. During a meeting the men generally sit in a circle of chairs. In the middle of the circle, on the floor, there is usually an assortment of ritual objects placed there by the leader. A small rug is often used to demarcate the center of the circle, often handmade in a Native American tradition. In the center of the rug is placed some kind of candle and candleholder, sometimes simple, sometimes quite elaborate. For instance, in Watani's group setting, one of his favorite implements is a handmade ceramic bowl from India full of sand with a small oil lamp in the center. Scattered around the rug are often handheld instruments like rattles, bells, maracas, drum mallets, and drumsticks. Some men own their own drums, and the leader maintains a collection of drums for men to use on nights that involve drumming.

The standard format of Watani's meetings is as follows. The night starts with Watani and whoever has arrived early setting up the circle. The members sit down and often begin by drumming and chanting. Both are essentially free-form, but the men make an effort to make their beats and chants consistent or at least compatible. Drumming and chanting may last about ten to fifteen minutes before Watani signals to the participants to wrap up. Next the men often do about ten minutes of Buddhist meditation. This may be followed by a brief ritual; a popular one is a Native American ritual in which they chant the phrase "hai ungawa" while turning to all four directions. This is meant to signify that one is "really here" in this one place and that one is also aware of the rest of the world in all directions.

After these preparatory rituals, the body of the meeting begins. Occasionally Watani will start off by talking about whatever holiday, ritual, or seasonal day is occurring according to any and all cultural calendars. In addition to standard Western holidays the group discusses non-Western holidays, for instance the Hindu celebration of the goddess Kali's birthday, and seasonal events like solstices. Watani does this to help "get the men in touch with" non-Western spiritualities, including a spiritual awareness of nature.

The group then proceeds to do "check-ins" in which each man talks briefly (for about one to three minutes) about the emotions he is feeling about significant aspects of his life as well as noteworthy things that happened in the time since the last meeting (meetings are generally weekly). The floor is then opened by Watani for any participant to speak about any significant emotional issue that may be on his mind. One of the men will speak, and the others will respond with follow-up questions, advice, and reflections on what the issues have to do with their own lives. On some occasions, the entire night is spent focused on one person and the issues that come up in relation to him. Other times the focus may be on two or more group members. One of the goals of this focus on one particular man at a time is to help that man explore emotions and identity issues at as deep a level as possible. Oftentimes what are seen as major breakthroughs occur, in which a man seems to discover things about himself and his life that he was not aware of before. Emotions often run high, including anger, sorrow (sometimes involving crying), and happiness. There is an emphasis on communal cohesion and respect for "one's fellow men." The meeting generally ends with a group hug, and Watani sometimes makes announcements about related events and speakers in the area. At that point, some of the men leave and others stay for a while and talk informally, sometimes further discussing issues that arose in the meeting.

The group meetings I participated in met at people's homes and in commercial locations rented by leaders. One location Watani used frequently was in a middle-class commercial area outside of the downtown area, in a building that was used for a small children's art school during the day. Meetings are always held in private, and any sources of interruptions or intrusions are avoided. The formal segment of the meeting is generally spent entirely in one room in a seated circle. But the periods before and after meetings seems to serve an important function also. During these periods members stand around and talk informally about such topics as events in people's lives, intellectual and spiritual ideas, news events, or recent movies and television shows. Members also sometimes choose to discuss and reflect upon what happened in the meeting, including issues that members want to explore more fully and perhaps discuss in more depth with particular other members. It is reasonable to conclude that the informal interactions are an extension of the more formal aspects of the group. Moreover, the informal nature of these interactions most likely helps maintain group cohesion by aiding in the construction of community through affective ties between members.

## MICROMETHODS OF SOCIALIZATION AND CONTROL

Watani is the "firetender/facilitator," as he calls himself, and is clearly the leader of his men's groups. He has taken on the role of emotional and spiritual teacher to the men. While some men follow his beliefs and suggestions more closely than others, he holds a significant degree of power over what transpires in his group each night. He uses this local group power through a number of different practices of microcontrol and persuasion. The data suggest he uses the following central practices: (1) the selection and initiatory socialization of new members; (2) the direct stating of group standards, rules, and values; (3) the reading of "instructional" poetry and stories; (4) the conducting of periodic rituals over which he has almost total control; (5) the controlling and altering of the direction of group discussions through several means; (6) the interrupting and sanctioning of breaches; and (7) the removal of men from the group. The following discussion of these issues serves as an introduction to some of the core ideological qualities exhibited in the group context. (Cultural beliefs and practices are explored in more depth in chapters 4 and 5.)

### Practice 1: The Selection and Initiatory Socialization of New Members

Each member's first experience of Watani as an organic intellectual/ socializing agent figure is their first phone call to him as prospective members. They have found a small flyer announcing his groups in an area alternative bookstore, community coffeehouse, or natural food store or on a public bulletin board. The flyer catches the eye with simply the words "Men's Groups" in large, bold, capitalized letters. It describes the groups as "Men Helping Other Men to Heal and Grow" and as offering "Support, Storytelling, Ritual, Therapy." It then quotes Robert Bly's *Iron John* (1990: 112): "I think what men need to do is to spread their wings in the valley of their own sorrow. . . . Get into a men's group, that's where your inner work is really done." With this text, the process of selection and socialization has begun. During the first phone call from a prospective group member, Watani begins to explain the fundamental principles of the groups in order to make sure that the man "is up to the challenge."

The first stage of admission is that of self-selection by each man; it is his choice to call Watani. This is most often triggered by the fliers and occasionally by recommendations from current members. After self-selection, the admission process is controlled almost totally by Watani. He impresses upon the men that they take on significant levels of responsibility by joining a group and that they will have to follow a number of central rules and norms. The function of Watani's warnings is clear: to weed out those who do not agree with the central principles of the movement, as he interprets them, so that they will not disrupt the smooth running of a group by contesting those elements that Watani considers incontestable.

Watani is very selective in his admission of new members, choosing only the men who are already most consistent with the movement ideology that he espouses.[4] He chooses men who already show some degree of belief in the idea that mainstream masculinity is flawed and who identify themselves as being critical of the effects of mainstream masculinity in their own lives. He also makes it clear that a prerequisite for being admitted into a group is being "ready" for the group, that is, already having a strong interest in and at least some ability for discussing emotional issues. Those who have previous experience with men's groups qualify immediately in this regard. Those with experience in psychological therapy aimed at personal growth tend to be seen positively, and men with a background in Buddhist meditation are also seen as good candidates. Those with no directly related experience are admitted if they show a high level of interest in discussing issues in their lives, such as being a better father, being a better husband, questioning their relationship to their career, finding greater happiness and satisfaction in their lives, or seeking greater spirituality. In the end, if the person does not measure up to the standards Watani chooses to impose, he will not admit the prospective member.

Watani pointed out the competitive nature of the application process when I was first accepted to join a group as an ethnographer. He had previously made it clear during a telephone conversation that I would have to join the group as a full member and that any observation I would do had to be in addition to being a full participant. At a one-on-one meeting he tells me, "So, you're in. I think you would work well with us. [*pause*] By the way, I just want to say that that's a real compliment.... You know, just to give you a sense of the thing, I maybe get eight to ten calls for every one person that I ask to come in for an interview. And out of eight to ten of those [interviewed], I only accept one person." While these numbers may well be exaggerated, it is clear that he has the opportunity to be selective in admitting new members into his organization. The result is that he has significant power to shape a group in his desired image prior to any interaction in the group itself.

After the process of member selection, in which Watani has been able to effectively exercise his power over the ideological vision of a group, he continues the process of initiatory socialization through direct explanation of central tenets of the group to new members. These are not presented as issues to be democratically discussed and agreed upon as a process of negotiation and consensus. Rather, they are rules, handed down from a position of essentially absolute authority in this regard. One example of this comes from my own initiation, as Watani explained the core value of "commitment" at our one-on-one interview meeting.

> Remember, if you can't make it any time, you have to call in. It's really an important issue. You need to be committed to the group. We all rely on each other. And if you can't make it, it needs to be for a good reason. Like one guy couldn't come because he was coming down with the flu. Or another guy recently had to do the bar exam. Or another wanted to be there for his kids who are in a school band and were performing. And that's where he had to be. He needed to be there to support his kids. That's completely right. He needed to be there as their father. So you can't not show up just because you don't feel like it or you came home from work and you're tired and fell asleep. If you do that, you buy the chair for the night, in other words, you pay anyway. We really need reliability in the group.

Watani works to construct me into his vision of the perfect group member, that is, the perfect grassroots participant in the men's movement.

It is interesting to see this technique of appealing to the interests of the group as a whole to support the legitimacy of this rule. Further, as part of this socialization process, Watani explains his formulation of a limited category of acceptable excuses for not attending. He has even instituted a monetary penalty for the violation of this central group norm of commitment.

After the stage of acceptance and initial socialization, Watani continues to mold new members on their first night in a group with the goal of creating new, fully functioning members of the men's movement. He does this by guiding the new member through the ritual aspects of the group process and further explaining the central values and norms. For instance, on Joshua's first night, Watani corrects him concerning the rules of ritual in the group. Joshua has violated a central principle, that actions must be done with "meaning," with "feeling," and not haphazardly. Watani points out the breach and enforces the local norm. In this case, Watani had cued Joshua to give out his food offering. Unsure of himself, Joshua produced a package of granola bars and he threw the first one across the circle to Greg. Watani stopped Joshua with a note of disapproval and explained that this is a ritual and must be done correctly, "with feeling and with heart." Watani explained that Joshua must be committed to what he is doing and instructed him to go around the circle and put a bar in each man's outstretched hand. Watani instructed Joshua in a quiet, yet commanding way. He wasn't angry, but he was clearly taking a strong leadership role here.

Watani's ideological shaping of new men during their first night in the group includes teaching the core value of listening. In explaining the check-in process to me at my first meeting, he emphasized this group tenet. This is part of his effort to encourage me to internalize the core discourse of the mythopoetic men's movement (which is explored in depth in chapter 4). Watani's teachings to new members also serve to reinforce for the rest of the members the importance of these aspects of the discourse. He explains the process of checking in, a ritual that happens at the beginning of each group meeting, explaining that each member starts by responding to the person before him. The man first shakes the rattle to say "I am here and I hear you who just spoke." He then explains that the man is to say something to the person before him that shows that he was really listening. "There's the highest percentage of quality of hearing in this group than you get in all the rest of your week." Watani explains that after checking in you hand the rattle to someone else, and he responds to you. Watani emphasizes that each man can hand the rattle to anyone, so every member always has to really listen.

Interestingly, Watani not only appeals to the cultural value of "really listening" but also includes a practical reason each man should listen well: a member could get the rattle at any time and be on the spot to respond to the previous person. This building of responsibility to each of the other men in the group is a key tactic used by Watani. It is a good example of an interactive strategy that is part of his continuing microcampaign for the spread of certain ideological teachings.

This first interactional practice of Watani's, the selection and initiatory socialization of new members, is one of the most distinct in terms of his power as a socializing agent and organic intellectual. For much of the process of this practice he is alone with the individual man, so the other members of his groups have no access to these interactions. Even during the process of initial socialization during a man's first one or two meetings, other group members almost always cede him the role of teacher of the new member. However, as my analysis unfolds, it becomes clear that Watani's authority is contested elsewhere and that outcomes are sometimes the product of group negotiation rather than top-down control.

*Practice 2: Direct Statements of Group*
*Values, Standards, and Rules*

It is clear that Watani exercises considerable power in shaping the group context through the selection and initiatory socialization of new members. Another very straightforward mechanism that Watani uses to try to achieve his goals as an organic intellectual is the direct statement of what he defines to be group values, standards, and rules. The previous discussion of Watani's rules about listening is an example of this as well as an example of the socialization of new members. In direct statements, Watani uses his authority to *tell* members how they should act. He presents his rules not as topics for discussion, something to reflect upon, or one possible way of doing things but, rather, as *the* way to be a member of the group. This mode of inter-action follows a pure authoritarian model of top-down command. While not every statement is followed completely and contestation does occur, for the most part Watani has a high level of success with this method. He has used the selection process to locate and include only those people who have the basic ideological orientation of the movement already, thus it is no surprise that the direct statements of general group tenets are rarely contested.

This technique of keeping a group focused ideologically by directly repeating and explaining central values is sometimes handled formally by reading from the "Group Workbook," a nineteen-page guide that Watani has compiled from outside sources and copied for each member. The booklet quotes movement high intellectuals such as Robert Bly and Sam Keen while borrowing mostly from Bill Kauth's 1992 movement text, *A Circle of Men: The Original Manual for Men's Support Groups.* Here is an example of a reading that Watani uses as an opportunity to remind the men in the group of the positive ef-fects that conflict can have. A group argument had obviously upset a number of members of the group, and Watani wanted to remind the men that conflict is not only acceptable but also a fully sanctioned part of the larger men's movement. He used the authority of his own "Group Workbook" and the words of movement high intellectual Bill Kauth to legitimate this point.

Conflict is a natural and important part of any relationship. The successful resolution of conflict will involve you and me telling the often hidden truth about why we want whatever it is we happen to want. In this open sharing, we come to know new aspects of each other. What is generally missing for us in our society is the safe space—the community—that supports our telling the truth at deeper levels. Your group is that opportunity. It is imperative that your group welcome conflict.

Watani supported the text with his own brief unscripted comment, explaining that he really believes what he just read. "Conflict is a good way for us all to grow together." He said that we build the group through this, not weaken it. This mechanism of direct statements of group values, standards, and rules is a regular tool in Watani's interactional arsenal. In later chapters I explore other examples of this technique of direct ideological construction.

### Practice 3: The Reading of Poetry and Stories to Indirectly Support and Encourage Desired Group Values

Another of Watani's techniques is the use of creative work by other intellectuals who may or may not be involved in the movement. Watani uses the evocative power of poets and fiction writers to evoke belief in what he considers to be important ideas, values, and codes of behavior for the men's movement. This is a more subtle, indirect process than the direct statement of group values whose internalization is framed as mandatory, as discussed in the previous section of this chapter. However, it is a key practice of Watani's promotional leadership, one that is clearly meant to help steer group judgment and categorization processes.

With creative texts, the men in the group are sometimes left to reach their own conclusions concerning the meaning and lessons of the work. On some occasions, the men directly engage the meaning of the reading and can offer alternative interpretations to those Watani may have originally desired. These kinds of readings are almost always discussed in terms of their relevance to the men's lives rather than in a more theoretical manner.[5] Watani generally uses them as points of reflection to add a desired perspective to an issue or set of issues that is part of the group process of discussion of personal matters. He will read them sometimes at the beginning of the discussion of a topic he has introduced as a means of focusing members' thoughts in a particular way before they begin to speak. Occasionally Watani will use a poem or story to try to refocus a discussion that he feels has gone astray. Other times he will conclude a discussion with a reading in a clear attempt to provide a focused conclusion to the interaction and perhaps give direction to members' further thoughts on the subject.

Watani explains his perspective on the utility of poetry in giving voice to feelings for men: "Other people's poetry is so beautiful that way. It expresses things we may not put into words ourselves. Some guys find it hard to say certain things themselves. They feel strange saying certain things themselves. So a poem might give a voice to something that's in them, and other guys will say, 'Oh, yeah, that really works for me too.'" This can be understood in terms of Gramsci's discussion of organic intellectuals being able to invoke in "the active man-in-the-mass" a "theoretical consciousness of his practical activity" (1971, 333). That is, people can be made to understand their practical, everyday experiences as concrete, real phenomena that are shared as a group. These phenomena can then be understood as explainable by certain specific theories and perhaps changeable through social action.

One poem that Watani uses as a tool to try to shape (or "raise") the consciousness of the men is "Transformative Ritual" by Gay Williamson (1994). This is a good example of a poem that attempts to bring out the unvoiced emotions of the reader. It also has the double function of serving to indirectly celebrate and legitimate men's groups themselves. It invokes central mythopoetic images of nature, fire, drums, the heart, and ancient wisdom. The poem attempts to invoke the emotions of pain, love, joy, and sorrow. It summons up the emotion-filled processes of trusting, reflecting, risking, and sharing. It talks about "the journey to new places within," referring to "the voice of the heart's soul." It is clear that this poem aims to invoke and stir the world of emotions, one of the central goals of men's groups discussed later in this chapter.

There are countless other poems and brief stories that Watani reads or has members read that call up similar images, exploring emotions in various ways and generally supporting the men's group ideology that Watani proliferates. Watani uses repeatedly a text he calls "the bible of the group," *The Rag and Bone Shop of the Heart,* a collection of poems and stories about men edited by Robert Bly, James Hillman, and Michael Meade (1992). Another central source is *A Path with Heart: A Guide through the Perils and Promises of Spiritual Life* by Jack Kornfield (1993). Watani had members buy this Buddhist book of philosophy, assigned certain readings from it, and used it extensively during group meetings.[6]

These creative texts often serve as jumping-off points for group discussion. During these discussions, Watani's direct socializing power is reduced. He can no longer control the interaction completely, and the top-down model has been transcended. Of course, the interpretation of any text is open to the creativity of each individual member, but the process becomes even more interesting when it becomes a cooperative effort on the part of group members and Watani takes on a secondary role. A good example is a discussion of the poem "Transformative Ritual."

Watani no doubt had specific lessons that he wanted to teach that this poem supported. However, interpretation of the poem became a bit more complicated than he might have expected when the discussion started. Stewart said that he likes the poem in general and that he definitely believes in the power of ritual, but that the poem is very vague. David joined in, saying that it seems like "a bunch of nice imagery, but what does it all mean?" Henry responded by saying that he thought the poem was "great" and that it really stirred up some emotions in him. He said that he needs work like this to "open up his heart" and get him "feeling in an honest way." Watani supported Henry's interpretation by saying that men need to learn to "risk openness" and explore difficult issues through ritual. David agreed but said that the group needs to do this in concrete ways, about concrete real things, not through "mumbo jumbo and New Age bullshit." Stewart agreed, saying that he wants to keep vague imagery to a minimum and get down to "real issues" in people's lives. Several men nodded to signal agreement, and Watani seemed a bit disturbed but agreed.

In this interesting and somewhat comical exchange, several men made clear their opposition to certain kinds of poetic expression. Watani's attempt to encourage certain ideals in the men, while certainly not a failure, did not proceed exactly as planned. Henry apparently received the text as Watani presumably desired, and Stewart supported the general teaching about ritual. However, the group staged a minor interpretive rebellion, suggesting that the reading of the poem in fact took away from the group's more important goals of dealing with real issues in men's concrete lives. This is a good example of the way in which Watani's power as an organic intellectual is never total. This exchange supports the idea that texts are always open to alternative interpretation and men can challenge Watani's presentation of them at any time. Thus, while the evidence suggests that Watani's reading of poetry and stories generally does support and encourage certain group values, it must be noted that the men can and do exert their individual agency in interpreting these texts. The meaning of corresponding interactions can never be totally controlled by Watani because meaning itself is the ongoing result of negotiated interaction.

*Practice 4: Conducting Targeted Rituals*

Rituals are a central part of men's groups. Each meeting is constructed around a broad, overarching, essentially unchanging structure. Within this formula is a place for periodic rituals. Watani has a high degree of control over which rituals are done, when they are done, and how they are done. He uses them as part of his promotional leadership to further pursue the political/personal socialization of group members. The general practice is to celebrate a particular event, most often a traditional Judeo-Christian holiday (Christmas, Passover), a nature-oriented or pagan holiday (summer solstice, fall equinox), or the birthday of a famous (generally Eastern) spiritual leader (the Buddha, Gandhi).

Each ritual episode involves Watani introducing the event and the men participating in some way, such as reading passages Watani gives them or some ritual action like putting a symbolic message into a small fire. Watani's introduction guides the men about the meaning they should attach to the event. It tells them what to consider worthwhile about this ritual and what lessons to take away from it. The men are then lead through the ritual through their own scripted participation. This participation serves to encourage deeper personal investment and emotional cathexis with respect to a ritual whose symbolic content Watani hopes they will internalize.

A good example of this process is Watani's use of Hanukkah to champion the resistance of oppression, celebrate the counterhegemonic power of organized peoples, and encourage political engagement. These are central themes within the mythopoetic men's ideology. At a meeting that fell on the second night of Hanukkah, Watani told a selective version of the traditional story of Hanukkah. He told the group that the Jews were persecuted by the Greeks, who wanted everyone to be Greek and to renounce any other religions in order to worship the true Gods, those in the Greek pantheon. So the Greeks discriminated against the Jews, killed them, restricted their religious practice, and took over most of their temples. After a while, Watani said, "the Jews said 'No more Mr. Nice Guy'" and they rose up and fought back. They had only primitive weapons, but they fought hard and eventually took back the temples and won back their freedom. The temples had been desecrated and partially destroyed, so they immediately set to work repairing them and making them proper holy places again. In the main temple, they could only find enough oil to burn for one day, but miraculously, it lasted for eight days, hence the eight days of Hanukkah. Watani declared that Hanukkah is a celebration of "the power of the downtrodden and the victory of the oppressed." As he stated, "At some point, if you keep pushing people, they're gonna push back."

As he always does, Watani continued by relating this traditional spiritual story to the present day. He said that it isn't "just an old story" and that we can see the same oppression in today's societies. For instance, he declared, Proposition 187 [the California anti-immigrant initiative that had just passed] is the same type of thing: "the dominant group of people trying to make everyone like them." He explained that this is a "racist move to maintain the position of a homogenous group of people in power." Watani directed the group to do check-ins oriented toward this story by discussing "times when you've been pushed back and didn't take it, times when you've fought either individually or been part of a struggle."

At this point the men discussed their own experiences with political activism and their own senses of justice and equality. This conversation went on for about an hour and seemed to be the kind of productive discussion that Watani encourages. Nonetheless, at one point one of the men interjected that he thinks the group should move on to other, more personal issues. He said he doesn't want to spend too much time "up in our heads" debating political issues that aren't directly connected to the experiences of the men in the group. This isn't "a political discussion group," he said, but a place to "share our souls" and get away from opinions and "pontificating." Greg agreed and said that he's really enjoyed the topic but that now it's time to move on to more personal topics. Stewart agreed, and he took the stick and put it in the middle of the circle.

Stewart's act of offering the talking stick to someone was a way of starting a new topic by inviting anyone in the group to talk about something important to them. This move ended the segment and the men moved on to another, unrelated topic. Nonetheless, Watani succeeded in his role as promotional leader; Watani's religion-oriented celebration served as an effective exercise in celebrating the importance of progressive political engagement. He succeeded in connecting a popular historical-religious discourse to practical political activity in members' lives, indirectly but distinctly connecting the issues of Hanukkah to the men's movement itself. Watani used not only his own authority but also that of the Judeo-Christian tradition to support and promulgate central men's movement political beliefs.

Nonetheless, this chain of events also shows that Watani's power as socializing agent is incomplete. Individual members can interpret what is occurring for themselves and seize control. While Doug, Greg, and Stewart did not undo the effects of the previous hour of interaction, they were able to avoid any further effects by ending the segment and moving on to a different topical focus. Specifically, they interpreted a continuation of the previous discussion topic as violating a group norm of concentrating on highly personal issues and avoiding what they interpret as purely intellectual debates. While Watani clearly thought the topic was appropriate, these three men were able to mobilize the opposing interpretation and change the focus of the group interaction.

Another example of Watani's use of traditional holidays to construct a ritual celebrating some of the core beliefs of the movement is a speech he made at a Thanksgiving dinner he organized with men from all of his groups. Watani commemorated the importance of family, community, and love as well as the importance of a kind of liberal, New Age, environmentalist attitude toward life and the natural world. He explained that he believes in the power of ritual itself and then got everyone involved by having each man speak in turn about the themes he has introduced.

Watani explained that he started having these Thanksgiving dinners several years ago because "we've lost the significance" of holidays in our culture, that almost all of "the meaning and the real ritual" has been lost. He said that we need to get that back in our lives and that that's what he had in mind for this event. He explained that a lot of people don't have "a big circle of people they really care about" to fully "experience the holidays the way they should be experienced." However, he pointed out, "we are a group of people who really care about each other" and thus we're perfect for a truly significant holiday get-together. Watani discussed reverence for food and for the life that it gives us, and he said we should be thankful to animals that have given their lives for us to eat. Later he gave thanks at the table to the turkey and chicken who had given their lives for the meal. Watani asked us to go around the table and give thanks for what we have in our lives. There was some joking, but the men seemed genuinely to get into the spirit of the ritual. They talked about their wives, girlfriends, children, and extended families and the resources that they feel fortunate to have in their lives. They talked about friends, "the light," "the music," and the other men there. It is clear that Watani has introduced and structured a ritual that succeeds at evoking and encouraging men's beliefs in family, love, and community and in spirituality in a broadly defined sense.

*Practice 5: Managing the Direction of Group Discussion*

Watani also exerts a considerable amount of control over the ideological direction of group interaction through the management of what is being discussed and the orchestration of who is talking. This is perhaps most clear in his presenting of topics for discussion. He regularly begins meetings by suggesting a theme about which the group will talk. While this is far from a perfect mechanism of control, it clearly gives Watani a privileged position vis-à-vis the content of group exploration.

As discussed in the previous section of this chapter, the running of rituals is one way in which Watani begins a focused discussion, and the reading of poetry and stories to introduce a particular topic is another. The simplest method, however, is to merely announce a discussion topic. Watani sometimes continues a topic from the previous week's meeting; this is almost always an option, because there is essentially always more that could be discussed related to a particular topic. Also, if there is a lull in discussion, Watani can return to the discussion of a previous issue. He can, therefore, choose and even return repeatedly to issues of his choice and, by extension, avoid or deemphasize issues that he sees as less important.

Another way that Watani manages the direction of group discussion is to end certain topics and switch to new ones by opening the floor to a random topic to be generated organically. He has only to say, as he often does, "Well, I think we've spent enough time on that. Why don't we see what else is going on for people?" Watani's topic change is sometimes contested, but generally he succeeds in ending one line of discussion and opening another. Alternatively, he can end a topic and open a directed line of discussion. For instance, one time I witnessed Watani thank Henry for "sharing" and for "being open to other men's input" about how he's handling his job search and the "feelings of powerlessness" that it brings up. He then suggested we move on to discuss our own "feelings of powerlessness" in the context of jobs and careers.

As is typical for Watani, he had processed Henry's testimony and ensuing discussion in order to select the themes that he wanted the members to consider further and to discuss in terms of themselves. He ended a broad, somewhat unfocussed discussion about Henry's job search and narrowed the discussion to people's "feelings of powerlessness" with respect to jobs and careers. The ensuing discussion explored in depth this central issue in the men's movement: how men's emotional lives are damaged by the masculine requirements of work and expectations of success in the public sphere (these issues are analyzed in depth in chapter 5). While the men in the group sometimes refuse to move on and insist on continuing the current topic, more often than not this practice succeeds in promoting a new topic.

Time is a resource that Watani draws on in concert with choosing or changing the topic as a way to manage the direction of group interaction. As the facilitator, he keeps track of the time and uses his position of authority to speed things up, slow them down, or eliminate them all together. References to time thus become another tool for Watani to do the socialization work of the organic intellectual. He can appeal to a time shortage to deprioritize or eliminate a topic or interaction and can also appeal to having lots of time in order to prioritize a particular subject matter.

On one occasion, an argument seemed to be starting immediately after another major conflict had just been resolved. It was getting late in the evening, and Watani likely wanted to end the night with a feeling of resolution rather than a feeling of division. It is his job to maintain a feeling of mutual support, caring, and community within a group. Not surprisingly, he snuffed out this potentially dangerous conflict by interrupting and saying that time was running out. He suggested that we could take the divisive issue up again another time, and he asked the group if there was any last thing that someone really wanted to say quickly before we finished.

Clearly the group was not actually *completely* out of time because Watani asked if anyone had anything else to say. He had succeeded at terminating a line of interaction that seemed likely to create discord and anger that could not have been properly managed at the time. Thus, it is reasonable to conclude that rather than take that chance, Watani seized the opportunity to close this topic and allow someone else to speak in what would, he hoped, be a less controversial vein. Again appealing to time, he made clear that it must be done quickly, before the end of the meeting. This guided any potential speaker not to open a difficult or large topic, thus steering the group in the direction of mutual resolution and communal closure.

Time is also invoked by Watani as a resource for socialization and control concerning the issue of repeating oneself. As an organic intellectual, Watani seeks to make the most effective use of the time with the members/recruits in his groups. He tries to keep his groups focused as much as possible on the issues that he sees as most important to growth and consciousness-raising. One way he does this is through appealing to time limits each night and thereby discouraging rambling and/or repetitious talk. He explained this to me directly during my initiation, and he regularly repeats this as a group rule during meetings. At one meeting I attended, Watani used this strategy to cut off George's line of discussion. Watani interrupted George and pointed out that George is repeating himself and that it would be constructive to move on. George accepted the point and then said that he thinks he repeats himself "because no one ever listened to me in my child-hood." He explained that he had to say everything over and over again in order to try to get someone to hear him. Watani commended him for acknowledging that. "You never got that out before. That's great to share that with us." The group then went on to explore this issue in George's life and in other members' lives. Watani's management paid off. In this particular case, not only did Watani avoid the loss of more time on a topic that he thought had run its course but also an entirely new, seemingly significant, issue was opened.

Watani's techniques of managing the direction of group interactions clearly demonstrate high efficacy in maintaining focus on what he sees as central group values and projects. Of course, as with most of his practices, this one is not always effective. Men can contest his interpretation of whether or not the topic needs to be changed; they can resist a theme that he introduces, suggesting alternatives or changing the topic again shortly; they can disagree about his assessments of the availability of time. This affirms the understanding that the ideological results of interactions are not solely the product of his social control but generally a negotiated outcome on the part of each participant exercising his own agency.

*Practice 6: Interruption to Sanction Breaches*

In pursuing his agenda of promotional leadership, Watani has a number of practices that draw on his role as group leader to maintain the norms and values that he has declared to be central to the groups' operation. He performs a policing function by maintaining those tenets and standards through not only repeated declarations of them but also the sanctioning of violations. This practice of enforcement both serves the goal of maintaining the particular ideological structure of the groups and can also be seen as a kind of unifying work, upholding a sense of common identity within the groups. This policing practice may also turn quickly into repair work in situations of conflict and/or threats to order. Dangerous antagonism can be mediated with appeals to group values and norms.

In one example of this sanctioning behavior, Watani chastised the group for neglecting to open up. Watani has defined "open sharing" as a central theme of the men's movement, one that is intended to counter what Watani and many others in the movement have identified as the practice of "hiding out" by men, that is, not sharing emotions openly. In this case, Watani attempted to trigger sharing by putting the speaking stick out for anyone to take. There was a very long pause, and Watani broke the silence by asking, "Who's sitting on issues?" After another pause he asked, "Who's sitting on issues, but won't admit it to the group or to themselves?" Watani attempted to inspire action by invoking the local taboo of hiding and indirect dishonesty through the phrases "won't admit" and "sitting on issues." If no one is speaking, then every man in the group is guilty of violating the rule of open sharing. Immediately after this interaction, Watani had to work even harder to get Tom to speak. After another long silence, Tom made a few motions and said "Um." Watani asked Tom, "Weren't you sitting on an eight-hundred-pound gorilla last week?" Following another long pause Watani asked, "Well?" Tom finally spoke on a topic of relevance to men's groups, but it had taken Watani quite a bit of policing effort to get the group working on an issue he deemed important.

Sometimes this sanctioning work has to be done very subtly, under very sensitive circumstances. A central goal of men's groups is to explore difficult and painful emotions as part of the directed change of consciousness of men. This can create very emotional situations in which the leadership work of policing is that much more challenging. In one instance, Talu was crying but not discussing what he is crying about. The crying itself is fully acceptable, in fact sometimes directly encouraged. What is not acceptable is to cry without also discussing the emotions behind the crying. Watani must carefully manage the situation. He asked, "What's happening right now, Talu?" He asked him where the tears were coming from. After a long pause Watani tried again. "Talu, open up." Watani told Talu that he's trying "to get you out." After another pause, Talu finally spoke, explaining quietly that he tends to "go down in this dirt hole" and pull a cover over himself and "zip it up and hide." Watani asked why he is hiding. Watani had succeeded in getting Talu talking, and the ensuing interaction found Talu exploring some very deep emotions about his childhood and his current life. Watani had achieved the goal of getting him to engage the other men and continue the focused work of the group.

While this policing practice is generally effective, it can be countered by the men in the group. The following exchange is a good example of this. Watani tried to get David to continue discussing a topic that he had been exploring with the group. David paused and then said that he thought he was done now. Watani tried to get him to continue again, but David got a little irritated and explained that he's really "gone deep with this" and needs to "process the emotions" before he's ready to talk about it more. There was a pause and then Nick jumped in and confronted Watani, saying that we should respect David's need to "give this time" and not force him to speak. The result is that Watani's efforts were thwarted, and the focus shifted.

In this interaction, Watani was trying to enforce the group commitment to very deep emotional exploration. But David resisted, arguing that he had achieved that general goal, and Nick combined forces with him, invoking a group belief in respect for other men and repeating David's claim to the need for time to further consider the issues. David and Nick mounted an effective appeal that did not seem to immediately pressure Watani to abandon his attempts but nonetheless succeeded in changing the topic shortly thereafter. While this exchange did not actually undermine the group's general belief in the importance of sharing emotions deeply, it did put limits on the strategy's execution and reined in Watani's power to enforce the practice without bounds.

A final related local norm that Watani enforces is that each man must speak from his own point of view; that is, rather than speaking theoretically and/or about others, members should speak about their own feelings and experiences. This is pursuant to the broader goal of getting men to "go deeper into themselves" and stop "hiding out." For example, Watani chastised George for talking in the "we" and the "you," not "from the I." "You know we try to avoid that," Watani said, and he explained that in his role as facilitator, he needs to help people "stay in the I."

Overall, in his role as organic intellectual and promotional leader, Watani has high levels of success in enforcing the group values and expectations that he has been pivotal in establishing in the first place. While his attempts can be contested, reinterpreted, or ignored, they tend to have the desired effect, that is, they keep the men focused on the ideology and goals of the movement. With a combination of persuasion and mild coercion, Watani succeeds at continually constituting a social movement organization on the micro level.

## Practice 7: Removing Men from the Group

Perhaps the ultimate policing action is to remove a man from a group entirely. In certain specific cases, Watani decides, in concert with other group members, that a man is disrupting the ideal operation of the group to such an extent that it is best to eliminate him from the group all together. Expulsion follows an extended period of attempts to get the man in line with the ideals and expectations that Watani has set for the group. If a member continues to not live up to his standards, Watani makes increasingly strong suggestions that he consider leaving; this is almost always followed by a departure that is framed as voluntary. It is only in an extreme case that Watani might directly terminate a member's involvement in the group without the man himself formally withdrawing first. Thus, when Watani gets someone to leave a group, it is almost never an explicit expulsion but, rather, a negotiated exit in which the man is generally persuaded that what he wants out of the group is not what the group can offer and that what the group wants out of him is not what he wants to offer. Thus, in one sense Watani is removing a man from a group; in another sense the man is being convinced to leave voluntarily. In this section I focus on the cases in which Watani initiates and pursues this removal process, as opposed to cases in which a man simply departs with no encouragement from Watani.

Over the roughly eight years of my research, Watani removed six members in one way or another. None of the men were removed because they dramatically differed with group beliefs concerning professed political ideology. Thus, none was terminated because he was too politically conservative, likely because Watani makes very sure that members are already in line with the basic ideals of the mythopoetic movement before they are admitted.[7]

The simplest violation for which Watani will encourage a member to leave is nonattendance. This breaks one of the first group rules that Watani tells each member: that members must "show up for your fellow men" and "show up for yourself." He made the importance of this rule very clear to me when I first began to attend the group meetings, and he has reported in interviews that this is one of the most primary rules. Moreover, Watani regularly reminds members of this rule in one-on-one interactions and during group meetings. "Men aren't taught to support other men," Watani has said. "You have to be there for yourself as well. It's easy not to come to group if you're tired and want to sit at home and watch TV, but you're selling yourself out when you do that. You don't just owe it to your fellow men; you owe it to yourself. You have to respect your process." So, Watani appeals to the needs of the group as a male community and to a member's own "need" to grow and develop as part of the member's "process."

Alex was removed from one of Watani's groups for poor attendance. He had missed two or three individual meetings without an excuse over a period of a couple months, leading Watani to chastise him during group meetings after each absence. Alex was absent several more times in a row without excuse, and Watani began to discuss openly Alex's removal from the group during meeting time and privately to me and to others. After a number of phone calls to Alex did not resolve the situation, Watani finally decided to remove him. As Watani told me a few days after his expulsion, "Alex just didn't have the commitment that's necessary. His heart just wasn't in it. It's too bad because I had real hopes for him. I thought he was really ready for this work. But what can I do with a guy who won't even show up even after all the calls and when he knows he should be here?"

Alex had repeatedly violated one of the most basic ideals of the group: that he show serious commitment to the group, to "his fellow men" in the group, and to his own "process" of growth. His lack of attendance is not depicted as mere forgetfulness or even as mere lack of interest but, in fact, as not being "ready for this work." He was judged not to be the right person for the mythopoetic men's movement.

Resistance to emotional exploration can also result in a member's departure from the group. The men have to be not only ready but also enthusiastic about sharing their deepest feelings. If Watani judges that a man is "holding back" and not participating fully, then Watani increasingly focuses on directly addressing this limitation in the member. If repeated urging over one or more months does not change the situation, Watani will encourage the member to leave the group if he is not willing to follow its precepts. This is precisely what transpired in half of the cases of removal that occurred during my research period, that is, in the cases of Ken, Victor, and Dennis. These three cases are very similar, so I focus here on just one, that of Ken, who stayed the longest of the three of them.

For several months before Ken was asked to leave the group, there was growing pressure on him to become more involved in group interaction. He was consistently the least talkative member of the group, and when asked about his life or otherwise prompted to participate, he often declined to respond or gave brief answers that were significantly less involved than typical responses. Ken was often encouraged during meetings to talk more and "go deeper." Watani and others called him on the phone repeatedly to urge him to get more involved. After a group meeting, Watani, Henry, and I discussed the situation. Watani said that he really wishes Ken would participate more in group, and Henry agreed, saying that Ken is "too closed off." Watani commented that Ken "puts up walls" and "hides out," "playing it safe so that he doesn't have to take any chances." I said that he seems "like a nice guy" but seems to "shut down" when things get "threatening." Watani said that if things don't change he would probably have to ask him to leave until he's really ready to participate more fully. Henry agreed that it's for the good of the group that Ken leave if he keeps this up. Watani said that Ken's attitude was really starting to drag the group down because "we're only as strong as our weakest link."

Watani, in concert with group members, is able to closely maintain a certain set of standards through the expulsion of those who do not reach them. This is a very conscious and strategic effort to keep up high levels of commitment and participation. It is clear that the effort here is not to amass the highest possible number of participants but, rather, to intensely develop a smaller number of men who reach high standards of growth in the direction of the new vision of masculinity. Henry displayed this orientation by supporting the removal of Ken. Watani makes it clear that the strength of the group must come before any individual member. Although significant effort is made to bring men into the fold, if ultimately they are not "ready for men's work" then their lack of engagement in movement ideals will eventually lead to their departure.

This same basic dynamic is exhibited in the removal of Joseph and Gabriel. They were also encouraged to leave because they were judged as ultimately not being appropriate for the men's movement. However, their attendance was perfect and the quantity of their verbal participation was high, so these were not the determining issues. They were removed for being overly hostile, angry, and defensive. This was interpreted as destructive to the group's identity and as another version of not being willing to participate fully and appropriately.

Joseph was a member of Watani's group for only six weeks, an unusually short period. On his first night, he made himself the center of attention, loudly interrupting, disagreeing, and complaining at great length about his life. He was chastised several times that first night by Watani and other members. They told him not to cut people off, and Watani told him that "attacking other men in the room" is not acceptable. Joseph was told that the point of group meetings is not to complain about life "in a surface, routine way" but to go as deep as possible into the emotions involved in one's unhappiness. As a longtime participant observer, I was truly surprised to see someone so out of sync with the group norms and values.

After that first night, Watani, Kevin, and I talked about Joseph. Watani said, "Boy, that Joseph's a real piece of work." I agreed and said he really had a lot to learn. Kevin said he didn't like him and thought he better "pull his act together" or "I'll throw him out myself." Watani said that we'd have to give him some time and try to get him to understand not to be "so hostile" and that "we won't let him cut everyone off." Kevin agreed, saying we can't let him turn the group into "Joseph's little bitching circle." In this case, Kevin was actually much more enthusiastic about getting Joseph to leave than Watani was. Nonetheless, Watani was clearly considering the issue.

In ensuing meetings, Joseph continued with this general mode of behavior, although to a somewhat less extreme extent. Multiple members urged him to respect other people more when they were talking, and Watani asked Joseph to mellow out a little bit with his criticism of men in the group. He explained that the group is not here to "coddle" men and that members do need to be questioned and held to task if they are not "doing their work" appropriately. Nonetheless, he explained, members need to really listen and try to deeply understand the situation before they offer alternatives and advice and that participation should not be in the form of "vicious attacks meant to wound." Members of the group agree with Watani.

Despite repeated efforts by Watani and others to change Joseph's behavior, he continued this pattern throughout his first six meetings. After increasingly severe warnings, Watani finally privately suggested to Joseph that he leave, and Joseph acquiesced. In an interview after Joseph had quit the group, Watani explained his interpretation of Joseph's behavior.

> Joseph used anger and hostility as a wall. He used them to try to keep his distance and maintain a safety zone.... A lot of men are like that. They keep anyone from getting close with all kinds of walls like anger and cynicism. He was also very defensive, as I'm sure you noticed. He couldn't take any form of criticism. Instead of accepting alternative suggestions as gifts that could be useful for him, he instantly jumped to defensive mind, taking everything as an attack that had to be defended against.... We just couldn't have that kind of energy in the room. The men have enough trouble with that kind of thing without having it thrown around group. We just can't accept that kind of thing or else everyone starts giving in to that temptation. All that anger, meanness, defensiveness, ... it was the same reason we had to get rid of Gabriel. No way we could keep that guy on either.

Watani clearly believed that Joseph and another member, Gabriel, were too hostile, angry, defensive, and disrespectful of other men in the group to qualify as members. They repeatedly violated central mythopoetic tenets and thus they were removed in one form or another. Again Watani was preserving a certain group identity through the practice of expulsion. Watani saw Joseph as a bearer of crucial polluted male traits (hostility, anger, defensiveness) that cannot be allowed to invade and infect the other men in the group.[8] He fears that if any member of a group is repeatedly allowed to personify the worst of these traits, then others are, by extension, allowed to as well. It is in this way that Watani uses his power to maintain and further develop the movement groups according to a certain ideological vision of counterhegemonic masculinity.

## CONCLUSION

Looking closely at the role of Watani, the leader of the Open Plain Men's Circle, helps us to develop a deeper understanding of the complex dynamics of ideological construction and consciousness-raising involved in this constituent element of the mythopoetic men's movement. The role of the men's group leader can be understood on a deeper level using the Gramscian concept of the organic intellectual, the active link between movement high intellectuals and the rank-and-file members that constitute a movement at its foundational level. Through the seven core practices explored earlier in this chapter, Watani pursues the cultural socialization of the men in his groups and in other movement contexts. Certainly his efforts at promotional leadership do not always succeed perfectly; the men sometimes actively contest, reinterpret, and rebuke his attempts. Nonetheless, the overall outcome is that he is able to define, disseminate, and maintain a certain specific set of ideas and standards through his collection of micro-practices of interactional power. This is a conscious, strategic effort to maintain high levels of commitment and action within the movement. Watani is developing a cadre of movement participants who will work toward the goal of a specific kind of counterhegemonic masculinity and a corresponding cultural and political consciousness.

## NOTES

1. The mythopoetic men's movement has traditionally been less centrally organized than other movements. Its generally decentralized mode of organization allows even more local control on the part of individual leaders.

2. For further discussion of these interaction dynamics, see Michener and Wasserman (1995).

3. See Lawler and Ford (1995) for an effective discussion of the dynamics of coercive tactics, particularly in conflict situations involving bargaining and interactional influence.

4. This raises the issue of competition *within* social movements between different organic intellectuals. There is a range of beliefs within the movement over which the organic intellectuals disagree, attempting in various ways to champion their own beliefs about the best movement ideology. The leaders can use their sway over local followers to spread their own interpretations of the high intellectual materials and ideals. This phenomenon was not a focus of this project, but it is certainly worthy of further research.

5. This is part of the group rule of only discussing issues that are directly, personally meaningful for men in the group. "Intellectualizing" and

"getting up in your head" is strongly discouraged. Thus general debates are negatively sanctioned and are immediately cut off if they are about anything other than issues of obvious immediate relevance to the actual lives of men in the group.

6. Other sources include Beck (1993), Bly (1990), Fields (1994), Kornfield (1994), Meade (1993), Mood (1975), Moore (1994), Moore and Gillette (1990), Suzuki (1993), and Trungpa (1984), to name a few.

7. Of course there are those who do not agree with the basic *tactics* of the mythopoetic men's movement, even if they agree with it in terms of general political ideology. These men are turned away from the beginning also, so the situation does not generally arise that a man has to be removed for that reason.

8. I explore fully what the mythopoetic men's movement considers to be the "evils" of traditional male identity, that is, the discourse of hegemonic masculinity, in chapter 4. Hostility, anger, and defensiveness are central characteristics coded as profane.

4

# Constructing
# Counterhegemonic Masculinity

This chapter examines the discourse of mythopoetic masculinity that constitutes the core ideology of the men's group context and partially constitutes each member's own identity. This discourse gives the members specific direction in their pursuit of this highly personal social movement. As part of this analysis, I construct and deploy a theoretical system of analysis that draws upon recent advances in cultural sociology. This theoretical approach enables a close examination of the ethnographic data, offering insights into the ideological processes and content that make up the mythopoetic men's movement.

I start with a discussion of the important theoretical issues that animate the analytical approach in this chapter. I explain the theoretical background behind the analysis of the empirical findings concerning the discursive dynamics of the critique of hegemonic masculinity and the construction of the discourse of mythopoetic masculinity. After this theoretical introduction, I turn to an in-depth analysis of the data pertaining to the men's ideological constructions, negotiations, and contestations. These data display the detailed codes that structure the discourse of mythopoetic masculinity.

## CULTURAL SOCIOLOGY

Recent work in cultural sociology (Alexander 1992; Alexander and Seidman 1990; Alexander and Smith 1993; Edles 1998; Jacobs 1996, 1998; Kane 1991, 1997; Sewell 1992; Sherwood 1994; Smith 1991,

1994, 1996, 1998; Somers 1992; Somers and Gibson 1993; Wagner-Pacifici 1994; West and Smith 1996, 1997) has argued forcefully for the need for more developed cultural thought in the face of reductionist and overly instrumentalist treatments of culture in social science, treatments that have left behind the autonomous role of meaning in social life. The history of cultural thought has led to this need for new developments in the field. Early cultural thought, from the 1940s to the 1960s, had a prominent standing in social science theory and research but came under a wide array of criticism pointing out a number of key weaknesses. This early cultural thought was attacked as a form of extreme idealism in which values were given an unjustified primacy over other types of social structures, and critics argued that the complexity and contingency of action was being largely ignored through the idealism of value analysis.

Despite the utility of these critiques, their voracity led to the opposing flawed conception: reductionism. On one hand, in an attempt to emphasize other noncultural social structures, culture was reduced to an adaptive, though creative and expressive, response to ecological and organization demands (Bourdieu 1984; Collins 1989; DiMaggio and Powell 1983; Wuthnow 1987). On the other hand, moves to solve the problem of action reduced culture to the product of immediate action and interaction or aggregate individual behavior (Garfinkel 1967; Goffman 1970, 1973; Pye 1988). Unfortunately, social science today is marked by the predominance of such social structural and actor-centered understandings of culture.[1] The contribution of these critiques is that they have produced more sensitivity to both structure and agency—that is, to such things as individual action, strategic motivation, noncultural structural causality, and social change—which has had some laudable empirical results. However, in their various forms of reductionism, these treatments of culture have ultimately sapped cultural dynamics of any real causal autonomy. I attempt to address this issue directly through a deep appreciation of the role of meaning. To address the problem of idealism effectively calls not for the rejection of a full treatment of meaning but, rather, for a better theory of the cultural system.

## CULTURAL DISCOURSE ANALYSIS

As part of the examination of the dynamics of the mythopoetic men's movement, I attempt to further develop a new strand of cultural theory, begun most prominently by Jeffrey Alexander and Philip Smith (Alexander 1992; Alexander and Smith 1993), that aims to address and grow from the previous criticisms of the history of the field. I begin with the definition of culture as "a structure composed of symbolic sets" (Alexander and Smith 1993, 156) constituting subjective meaning, values, social narratives, and, indeed, identity itself. Symbols are signs that are collectively shared, serving to instantiate meaningful categories for understanding the elements of social and individual life. A nonmaterial structure is then constituted through the interrelation of these symbols. Patterned order in social action is created from and constantly recreates this ideational structure. It is thus a product of collective action, simultaneous with its shaping of collective action. Of course, no one individual's action creates or is perfectly determined by this structure.

This large-scale structure is constituted at a more basic level by microstructures as described by Saussure (1985). The meaning of a sign does not arise from an objective, direct relationship with material reality, as in standard positivist assumptions. Rather, meaning is drawn in relation to the other symbols in the system, through similarity and difference, in relations of binary pairs. Thus, other signifiers, not the object of focus (the signified) serve to endow any particular sign with meaning. The system of meaning that is a group's culture can therefore be seen as a "web of intertwining sets of binary relations" (Alexander and Smith 1993, 157).

Discourses, like the discourse of mythopoetic masculinity, are symbolic representations that serve to communicate information in a cognitive sense and in significantly evaluating the object of focus. This infusion of value occurs through the moral attachment of binary sets to the quasi-religious fundamental categories of the sacred and the profane (Durkheim 1961; Eliade 1957, Shils 1975). Thus certain referents (actions, individuals, groups, processes, objects, institutions) are imbued with purity and others with pollution (Douglas 1966). Individuals are motivated to protect the pure, the good, the sainted, and to defend against the polluted, the bad, the demonic.

This process of discursive structuring is seen in the construction of the binary set of liberational masculinity and hegemonic masculinity. As I explore in depth later in this chapter, the members of this movement construct a complex, structured image of what they see as bad about traditional masculinity while they simultaneously construct what they see as the opposite, liberational masculinity. A deeper understanding of the underlying dynamics of the movement can be gained through using this model to analyze the observed data. It is these discursive understandings of the social world that direct, motivate, and constitute the movement itself.

The discursively animated evaluative process I just discussed is absolutely central to the understanding of cultural-ideological conflict. Culture is charged with these commitments of sacredness and profaneness, goodness and badness. Conflict is thus necessarily cultural in part, given the internal structure and logic of culture itself. In fact, repression, exclusion, and domination are necessarily central to the evaluative system. Given this conceptualization, a society without any ideational conflict, discord, or battle is a nonsensical concept. Pollution, transgression, and purification are ritual processes, integral to the dynamics of social life (Alexander and Smith 1993, 158; Stallybrass and Whyte 1986; Turner 1969).

At a less emotionally charged level, discourses also serve to make sense of the most important structures and processes of social life. This definitional, sense-making character of a discourse also serves to regulate these central components of society. Thus, the nature, dynamics, and justifications for kinds of equality and inequality are contained within certain public discourses. Deviance is understood and punishment justified through discourses. In short, actions, structures, and institutions are made sense of by members of society through their participation in the relevant discourses. These discourses are economic, political, religious, scientific, military, historical, personal, and more (Alexander and Smith 1993, 10).

We must therefore dispense with the misconception that an idealized, symbolic system of signifiers must necessarily be limited in effect to the ideational realm. In constituting our very understanding of all the components of social life, both symbolic and material, the discursive code is intimately involved in all social action, having a mediating and structuring role in all of social life. In fact, at a fundamental level understanding cannot occur without an internally logical discursive structure. The meaning of symbols and representations would be random, ceasing to have any causal significance for action.

It is important to appreciate that culture and its components must be understood as both internalized *and* externalizable/changeable. Culture structures (for instance, discourses) are believed in to some extent by the members of the relevant community and thus impossible to completely remove oneself from. As a member of a particular symbolic community (such as the mythopoetic men's movement), one is partially constituted in terms of one's own identity by the relevant culture structures. But at the same time members can at least partially see culture structures and understand them in certain ways that allow strategic action with respect to them. Thus, the discourse of mythopoetic masculinity, while having a general structure that transcends any individual short period of time, is still at any moment subject to potential criticism, negotiation, and reconfiguration.[2]

Recent empirical research in sociology has found cultural discourse analysis to be quite effective at understanding data in a way impossible with other approaches (Alexander 2003, 2006; Edles 1998; Jacobs 1996, 1998; Kane 1997; Magnuson 1997, 2005; Rabinovitch 2001; Smith 1994, 1998; Wagner-Pacifici 1994; West and Smith 1996). I take as my specific jumping-off place the work on the discourse of American civil society begun by Alexander (1992) and Alexander and Smith (1993). This framework focuses on the sacred and profane across the axes of motives, social relationships, and social institutions. In my research, I have discovered that the discourse of mythopoetic masculinity that is constituted through interaction in the men's group context has two halves, that of the new masculinity code and that of the traditional or hegemonic code. The two are positioned as binary opposites, one essentially the mirror image of the other. Thus liberational masculinity constitutes the positive and sacred evaluations of motives, social relationships, and institutions and hegemonic masculinity constitutes the negative and profane evaluations. Together they compose one discourse.

A certain kind of social-psychological makeup is seen as necessary for embodying a certain masculine discourse. To be sure, there is as much psychological variety as there are individuals, but there are a number of broadly defined normative commitments that define different kinds of masculine identity. As I explore later in this chapter, men who embody a certain set of motivations in their lives and are involved in certain qualities of social relationships are criticized by the mythopoetic men's movement as being dupes of hegemonic masculinity. Social institutions are likewise evaluated within the discourse. Institutions are criticized if they are composed of certain kinds of men and characterized by certain institutional qualities. And of course the converse holds for the positive discourse. Men with motivations and social relationships that are opposed to the profane side of the discourse are praised for being part of (or consistent with) liberational masculinity. Institutions marked by fulfilling the counterhegemonic code are correspondingly evaluated positively.[3]

The ethnographic approach I use in this book is a methodological contribution to Alexanderian cultural discourse analysis given its tendency to focus on written texts as its empirical data. Examining dialogical texts of verbal interaction allows me to take a closer look at symbolic meaning as it is being constructed in the creative moment of action. This approach makes possible a rich understanding of symbolic production and its effects as the actors are seen debating meaning in the real time of situated interaction. Understanding the dynamics of meaning creation on this level of detail and spontaneity is impossible in the analysis of traditional, monological text. This book thus contributes to the growing body of work that is developing cultural sociology both theoretically and empirically by reworking it with sensitivity to microlevel foci (Eliasoph 1990, 1998, 2002; Eliasoph and Lichterman 2003; Grazian 2003, 2004; Grindstaff 2002; Hays 1994; Lamont 1992, 2000; Lichterman 1995, 1996, 1998, 1999, 2002, 2005; Swidler 2001).

## THE DISCOURSE OF MYTHOPOETIC MASCULINITY

In uncovering the discourse of mythopoetic masculinity, I examine what are perhaps the three most fundamental topical foci of the mythopoetic men. These themes recur repeatedly in the men's interactions and are central to the constitution of group identity and the identities of the individual men. These three empirically defined foci are (1) the ongoing construction and maintenance of a common cultural space for interaction, (2) the construction of a general critique of mainstream American/Western culture, and (3) the construction of a counterhegemonic masculinity and a corresponding critique of traditional, hegemonic masculinity. In other words, members of the mythopoetic men's movement create a space for their ideological work and then they do it, in two primary ways: they criticize society in general and gender and masculinity specifically, and then they construct alternatives. This is not only what they do but who they are; this is the group identity, and it is also part of each man's own individual identity.

Looking at these issues, one can gradually distill from the data the exact, minute dynamics of the culture structures being constructed, mobilized, contested, and changed through naturally occurring, situated interaction. A complex structure emerges that I refer to as the discourse of mythopoetic masculinity. I explore the microinteractional processes that are the creative source of this discourse, a cultural resource that is alternatively embraced, rejected, adjusted, and fought over. In the end it is important to understand that this complicated and messy ideological process is precisely the process of creating and *doing* this unusual social movement.

### The Ongoing Construction of a Common
### Cultural Space for Interaction

Perhaps the most basic and necessary work being done by the men in this movement is the creation of a local cultural space in which they can interact as they see fit. This space must have some set of agreed-upon ideals, standards, and rules of engagement. This minimum base upon which all other interaction is based has a certain continuity over time, but it is always open for debate and refiguration. The construction and maintenance of a common cultural space is an ongoing achievement, an ideological process that is messy and challenging. The result is a continuing institution that can be referred to as a mythopoetic men's group.

The men's socially constructed, local cultural space is characterized in general by a commitment to what they see as openness, safety, and communality. The members are actively involved in constructing and maintaining an institution that meets their definition of a supportive community. A central tenet is that the men's group context is "a safe space" for the airing of personal and sometimes highly sensitive emotions and concerns. The building of trust and faith in one's fellow group members is seen as an absolute necessity for this. Thus the group context is constructed to be a communal association of equals, a place where people are committed to each other's welfare and growth.

The men's group context is built to be a specific zone for the creative and open expression of emotions and exploration of personal issues. For example, Nick made this clear when he stated, "What I like about the group is that we just get to hang out together and be real. It's not often you get a group of men where you can just be honest and open on a deep level and know that you'll get support in that." Mario made a similar statement: "I need to feel safe in this group. If I'm gonna open up and really deal with the hard stuff, then I need to know I can trust these guys, you know. I think everyone agrees. No one wants to get attacked in that asshole way that says 'I'm better than you,' that tries to cut you down so the other person can feel better about himself. . . . So when criticism happens, it has to be constructive; it needs to be done in a way that's trying to help the other person grow."

Terrence painted a picture of what draws him to his men's group:

> I come here to really get heard and supported in ways that I often can't out in the rest of my life. Other men are so often closed off and afraid of their emotions. I often feel like I'm not supported in

being emotional, that I have to be careful what I say or else people
will think I'm weird. Either that or I have a conversation about
something deeper than sports and the news, but it just doesn't go
that far. It stops at a certain point.... I find that I just can't rely
on other men when it comes to emotional stuff. That's what this
group is for: a place to be honest and to be with men that you can
trust and who are ready to deal with deep emotions.

Mario, Nick, and Terrence articulate sentiments that typify those
of other members I saw in countless meetings and interviews. They
want a place to go where they can be with men who are also ready
to explore emotions and who are ready to construct a close, intimate
group of fellow explorers. In other words, they want a place where
they can construct social relationships based on the codes of emotional
openness, supportiveness, and trust. They want their men's group to
be an institution marked by emotional safety and a communal spirit
of togetherness.

A fundamental characteristic is the desire for the men's group
to be a place where members can be honest and not afraid to talk
about potentially embarrassing issues. Watani made this clear from
his own perspective, saying that the group is a place for men to "let
your *tzitzit* show." He explained that when he was a kid growing
up, the orthodox Jewish kids would be wearing prayer shawls under
their clothes and that sometimes the tassels of the shawls (the tzitzit)
would slip out of their clothing and other kids would make fun of
them. He explained that in the group men wouldn't be "shamed"
for embarrassing things. He said that the group is a "safe space" for
everyone to "let it all hang out." "We're a family here," he explained.
"We're a group of men who care." Watani counterposes the group
context with the broader social world by explaining what the group
is not—it is not a place where anyone who is unusual is supposed to
be criticized, where anyone who deviates from the dominant norms
is teased and condemned. Instead, it is seen as a close community,
a place to be supported in potentially embarrassing and dangerous
emotional work. In Mario, Nick, Terrence, and Watani's comments,
one sees the structure of the negative side of the discourse beginning
to emerge simultaneously with that of the positive side.

Faith and trust are central tenets of the men's discourse. These
values are seen as necessary for the construction of a circle of men who
feel that it is safe to take chances within this context. Watani builds
this into the ritual initiation ceremony, which each new member goes
through. Watani leads the new member into the room with his eyes
closed and walking backwards. As he explains, "You are really entering

blind. You won't know any of the guys and it's an act of faith. We'll drum you in and I'll sit you down. It's total immersion and trust." Part of the initiation is also to bring something small but personally relevant to offer the fellow members to eat as a way of extending them well wishes. Watani discussed this with me. "One guy brought this kind of special cashew that he really likes. Or another guy brought cherry tomatoes that he had grown himself. Something that is significant for you, something to share with the guys and say, 'Here is something that's part of me in some way.' Something that is comforting for you that you feel good about.... And each of the guys will just automatically put it in their mouth. It's an act of faith."

Anthony articulated a similar idea, but in different terms.

> When I walk in that room, I know that these guys are here for me. I know that I can trust them and count on them to listen to me and try to help me, whether that means agreeing with me or disagreeing with me. I want to be able to relax and just be around a good group of guys who are really there for me.... So many people in the outside world are ready to judge you all the time. But they're not doing it out of love. They just don't have faith and real compassion.... I want them [the guys in the group] to be supportive but also to tell me when I'm full of shit.

Anthony asserts the same codes of supportiveness and trust as the others, and he also makes the important point that supportiveness does not mean always agreeing with someone. The men want suggestions, advice, and constructive criticism. They want to open themselves up and discuss issues with which they are having difficulty, precisely in order to get advice and guidance from fellow men. They want a safe, communal environment in which to do challenging emotional exploration.[4]

Members see the group context as a kind of special site centered around a commitment to shared values. This involves a mixture of seriousness and humor, but there is a concerted effort to make sure that everyone is doing "their work," and collectively doing what they refer to as "the work" of a men's group. The "work" is the growth and exploration that is the focus of the group context. If members feel that group interaction has gotten off track from this goal, they raise the issue. A perceived violation of the discourse is often identified and criticized.

In one case, Scott felt that members were violating what he sees as the purity of the men's group space by drinking wine. He rushed across the room to them and said, "Wait, stop! Don't drink." He challenged the men, saying the "work," the "ritual" needs to be done without drinking. He said he wanted to maintain a "sacred space." This drinking of wine was taking place at a special Thanksgiving gathering; Watani calmed down Scott, who later apologized for becoming what he called inappropriately doctrinaire. Nonetheless, the men who were drinking apologized for disrupting "the space" for him and agreed that in the future the members should all agree about the nature of these special events so that this kind of confusion and disruption would not happen again. There is an agreement that some mythopoetic events are more sacred than others and that in some cases drinking, for instance, would be inappropriate. Thus, the difference between the men here was over the nature of this particular event, but the entire interaction was couched in terms of their agreement on the general sacrality of "men's work." This underlines the importance of the nature of the space, of its "specialness." Scott, Watani, and the others all want to be sure that everyone works together to create what they define as a sacred, communal space.

I have thus far uncovered the beginning of the structure of the discourse of mythopoetic masculinity that these men are constructing.

*The Construction of a Critical Alternative to Mainstream American/Western Culture*

As shown in the previous section of this chapter, the men's group context is seen as a space separate from the rest of society. Specifically, the men's group is seen as representing a critical alternative to the rest of society. Members portray the society around them as having a number of debilitating flaws that adversely affect them, and the group context becomes a site to collectively discuss and formulate criticisms of that outside society based on personal experience. Further, group interaction is a resource used to address the ills that members see in themselves, injuries that are often seen as symptomatic of the problems of the larger culture. In short, the group context is a site for an ideological counterformation: members see it as an alternative microsociety, a separate community in opposition to mainstream America and what they see as its profane, flawed nature.

Values and principles that are seen by the mythopoetic men's movement as critically resistant to many of the perceived problems of society are freedom, openness, love, spirituality, ritual, honesty, listening to others, being heard by others, empowerment, and respect. American/Western society is variously portrayed by the men's movement as constricting, oppressive, unloving, unspiritual, close-minded, individualistic, and disempowering. These criticisms are expressed sometimes in a more intellectually rigorous way and at other times in a more "commonsense" way.[5]

The men's group is seen as a place for members to relax and be honest, free of certain constraints that they feel are prevalent in the rest of their life. The group context is seen as a zone of freedom, apart from the limiting control of the everyday world. The men see themselves, at least in part, as living under a dangerous hegemony, living in a world that continually damages them emotionally; the men see themselves as being subtly controlled and constrained by this hegemonic culture.

Before a group meeting started one night, Greg discussed with me his ideas concerning the differences between a men's group and the rest of society. He started by commenting that it is "so lame" that another member, Doug, comes to group in a tie and dress shirt and pants. I asked whether Doug comes to group directly from work, and Greg said he does, but that Doug could at least "take the God-damned tie off!" Greg expressed amazement that anyone would wear a tie to a men's group, because the group is a place to relax and "to forget about that kind of stuff." Talus joined the conversation, and he and Greg suggested that public life in American society is often a big restrictive game in which one has to follow other people's rules. However, at the end of our discussion Greg suggested that there are strategies of resistance that can be used in the face of such power. He said that you just have to play by the rules sometimes, that you have to do what they tell you to get what you want sometimes, and Talu replied that it's all a kind of game where you have to play along most of the time. Talking about ties again, Greg said, "What the hell is this strip of silk that we wrap around our neck? It's so stupid." Greg said he has a couple of "funky" ties that he likes to wear when he's expected to wear a tie for something other than work. "Yeah, you gotta let 'em know that you don't believe in their rules."

Greg makes clear what he thinks about conformity to restrictive rules laid down by those in power. He suggests a binary image of "us" versus "them," where "they" have power and "we" do not, where "they" are uptight and "we" are relaxed, where "they" demand compliance and conformity and "we" demand individuality. He suggests that it is useful to follow rules in some instances, but that when possible one should resist "their" control. It is not a very well-developed or informed theory, to be sure, nor does it have a vision of social change. However, Greg does develop the ideological imagery of power and control as well as concepts of how to manage that control through resistance to deference. This is the core imagery of hegemony and counterhegemony.

One of the specific rules of American culture that the men's movement identifies as problematic is that of not being able to express oneself openly. The group is seen as avoiding this kind of emotional control over individuals. As George declared, "I need to be free here." He said this is the one place where he feels he can be free and say what's on his mind. Later that same night, talking outside after the group meeting, Carl, Greg, and I discussed feelings of restriction in mainstream society in terms of emotions, specifically anger, and the emotional dishonesty that individuals are forced into by the rules of dominant culture. Carl complained that there are so many "parts of society telling us to be quiet," to "not show anger," and "that's wrong." He said it's too restrictive and that it sometimes "drives me crazy." He explained that he really doesn't want the group to fall into this pattern. I agreed, saying that "peace, love, and understanding" are important but that they only go so far, that people have to be angry when they're angry. "We have to be honest." Greg agreed, explaining that it's like a lie to oneself and to others when one is angry and suppresses it.

Men's group members identify society's emotional restrictiveness as a "normalizing" force that pressures individuals into conformity with the dynamics of hegemony. In one exchange, the members of one of Watani's groups criticized the hegemonic culture for labeling those who do not fulfill the dominant codes as deviant and strange, as problematic and profane. George and Doug discussed this in their check-ins, and others agreed. George said he'd been feeling pretty good lately. He retold a story from the past week in which he realized that some people think he's "a little weird." He smiled and said that people at work, his family, and some friends think he's "a little different." He declared that he likes it that way. "Here's to being weird!" There were nods and sounds of agreement around the room. George paused, then shook the rattle and handed it to Doug. Doug shook the rattle and shouted, "All hail weirdness!" He smiled and said that weirdness is "in us all."

Group members often depict the dominant culture as lacking a full sense of beauty, love, and spirituality. Typical members of mainstream society are seen as uptight, close-minded, controlled, and coldly rational. They are seen as closed off to their own subjectivities, closed off to what is depicted as the true complexity of their own consciousness. Watani told the story of a retreat he attended in which he felt the group of therapists he was with were trapped in this way of thinking.

Well, I went to this therapist weekend type of thing this past weekend and it was pretty bad.... One thing I learned at it is not to go to these types of things. I mean, it was so dry, so scientific; there was no soul, no sense of myth, or beauty or feeling. It was just a bunch of licensed therapists and people like that that have no sense of poetry, of the wonder of life. I got a few people to go with me who do drumming, who do more spiritual stuff and that was good, but it was just us. They gave us a slot in the morning and that was it. So we drummed for like an hour in the morning and that was the end of it. The rest of the time was speakers, meetings, and then it all ended with a big meeting in this huge cold lecture hall where all they were talking about was how to get more people to come next year.... I mean, all the magic had been sucked out. All those people with their clenched sphincters! They're all head, with no heart.

Watani expresses the difficulty he has outside mythopoetic men's events in developing what he sees as a fully spiritual approach. He sees these retreat attendees as uptight and overly rational, as oriented to social relationships marked by being emotionally closed off, distant, and unloving. He sees the atmosphere of this conference as marked by habit and drudgery instead of spontaneity, by conformity instead of individuality.

Another issue in which group members seem to orient themselves in opposition to a perceived dominant culture is that of listening well to others and being heard by others. Members particularly complain of "not being heard" in their families growing up. The men's group context is understood to be a place where quality communication can take place and people pay deep attention to each other. Watani made this very clear as he explained his group prior to my admittance. "There's the highest percentage of quality of hearing in this group that you get in all the rest of your week, or month, for that matter." He explained that that core feature of the group corrects for the poor listening skills that most people encounter in themselves and others. Watani clearly has the notion that the group is breaking from the dominant mode of interaction on this issue and creating an alternative.

This issue of being heard comes up regularly as an important value, one that is seen as opposed to the dominant culture. The men's families are a particular target on this point. Greg said that he "always had problems getting heard" when he was young; he told the group that his parents were very busy all the time and that he felt like they never really listened to him. "I think that's behind a lot of pain," he stated.

George appealed to the group to treat him differently than the pattern that he sees from his childhood. He explained that he thinks he

repeats himself because no one ever listened to him during his childhood and that he consequently needs "people to hear me here."

Quality listening is a discursive code that if breached will be
enforced. In an angry interaction between John and Scott, tempers
flared and Watani interrupted. He thought Scott was attacking John
unjustly and not realizing that John was in a lot of pain over the issue
they were discussing. Watani questioned Scott by asking whether he
was "really listening" to John, whether he sees that John is "hurting." John took up this point, somewhat angrily telling Scott that he
doesn't think he is really listening. John then tried to explain to Scott
exactly what he had been saying. Later in the same exchange, William
brought this point up again, suggesting that both John and Scott feel
that they are not being listened to and that that is a significant issue
in the conflict. William said that what he hears from one side is "I
need to be heard. I can't believe you're not listening to me." And he
said that what he hears from the other side is, "I need to be heard. I
can't believe you're not listening to me."

In these interactions, there is a clear commitment to the idea
that group members must be motivated by concern for their fellow
members, motivated to be attentive and communicative. Members
depict ideal social relationships as emotionally close, concerned, and
interactionally respectful. Their families and the "outside" world in
general are portrayed in part as falling dangerously into the binary
opposite of this ideal, as distant, neglectful, unloving, and uncom-
municative.

While the focus of the group is usually personal and emotional,
on some occasions members mobilize a systematic and generalized
critique of modern society as something that needs to be opposed
and fought against through political involvement. Watani, Scott, and
David specifically labeled society "capitalist" in a critical way. This characterization is generally explicitly or implicitly accepted by the other
members, and it has certainly never been opposed. Consistent with
the emerging discourse of mythopoetic masculinity, Watani and Tom
portrayed political struggle as ideally a community activity marked by
a collective spirit. Watani presented his views on these topics, talking
about his political involvement in the 1960s, describing the development of a "community of struggle" that was very cohesive and very
satisfying. He said that that is lost today and he misses it. "I've been
fighting my whole life" in mainstream society and in the men's movement, he said, and he is completely fed up with "capitalist, consumer,
fantasy society." Tom expressed similar concerns, saying that he is disappointed in the loss of the political spirit of the 1960s. David made
a very strong political pronouncement against capitalism: "I've never

understood capitalism.... [It is] an inconceivably horrible, ridiculous system." Members of the group laugh and nod in agreement.

Some group members are clearly enthusiastic about being involved in political struggle as a public, collective activity targeted against what they see as a generalized system of injustice. Some bemoan the difficulty of active resistance and/or present themselves as disappointed in their own lack of involvement. William explained problems with his more personal battles. "I fight every day of my life," he said, and described conflict with people related to his work, with his parents, and with others. He said it is very exhausting. Tom, discussing his past political involvement, reported that at this point in his life he is supportive but uninvolved. He said that he wishes he was more involved in political struggles today, but that his family responsibilities keep him away from that to a large degree (he is a divorced, single father with two young children). David made a similar point about how his political activities have been somewhat limited lately, but he said that he has been very proud of several things, including an antiwar play that he produced and acted in during the [first] Gulf War and when he did Hunter S. Thompson's *Fear and Loathing in Las Vegas* during the [Reagan-]Bush era. Carl dramatically portrayed his regret over lack of involvement, saying "I'm ashamed of myself" for not being more politically active. He discussed how he had been "narcissistic" and had been "floundering" for so much of his life. Interestingly, part of Carl's reported shame is most likely due to his comparing of himself to his contextual understanding of the rest of the men as being politically committed and active.

Some of the group members' criticism of today's society is targeted specifically toward work and the business world. Greg discussed his problems with money and he spoke very generally about "the system," without any further explanation. "You know, it's the system. Like, I have to go to work everyday and schlep around and do this crap just to make money and I hate it, but I have to pay the bills.... I don't have any choice. I have to do this crap work just for money." After a group meeting, William and Scott discussed problems with the work world in terms of it being overly "competitive," concerned with "goals and achievement" and involving morally judgmental evaluations of workers. William declared that people get "so uptight" about things in the world, that, for instance, at work people are "so businesslike" and that they're "so rational" and so "into goals and achievement." Scott agreed, saying the idea is "Let's go out there and achieve." He criticized "all the competition" and said that everyone acts like "I'm right; you're wrong," like they know the best way to do things and if you don't do it their way, you become a "bad person."

In keeping with the overall focus, political issues are almost always discussed in personal terms, rather than abstract, theoretical terms. This can take the form of defining political activity as more local to one's immediate everyday life, as William did. Or it can take one of the forms that David expressed, participating in a less obvious form of protest (in his case, putting on a play, Hunter S. Thompson's *Fear and Loathing in Las Vegas,* that is not overtly political but nonetheless undermines certain perceived norms of the social climate at a particular time). In fact, this definition of the group situation as explicitly personal and emotional *as opposed to* intellectually political was at one point raised explicitly by William. Watani had directed the group to do check-ins by discussing "times when you've been pushed back and didn't take it, times when you've fought either individually or been part of a struggle." William responded to this idea critically, saying that he feels like the group is being pushed to be political instead of "doing our work," which is more emotional and personal. Watani argued that what he had proposed does fall within the bounds of group work, that he is asking not about opinions but about personal experiences and what these things have meant in the men's real personal lives. There was no further discussion of the issue and William did not respond, so Watani's argument "won" by default.[6]

In the men's group conversations I have reported thus far in this chapter, there is a clear orientation to the mainstream world as profane and symbolically polluted in key ways. While members disagree about the details of some of these critiques and vary in their degree of radicalness on specific points, there is certainly a general commitment to some kind of critical progressive orientation. In terms of the discursive codes that arise, we see that the general population is portrayed here as motivated by impersonal, overly rational goals. They are seen as forming social relationships that are judgmental in the context of competitive institutions like the work world and society in general. The social world is portrayed as fundamentally unjust, as demanding conformity under a generalized system of control. The American political system and society in general as institutions are negatively identified as capitalistic and oppressive, necessitating counterhegemonic activity. The men have no specific plan for bringing about counterhegemonic change on the macro level and thus are not political activists in the usual sense. Instead, they have an unusual agenda of personal change and local cultural change.

In this section I have uncovered further elements of the discourse of mythopoetic masculinity that is being constructed by the men.

Many of these discursive findings are further supported and explored in the next section.

### *The Construction of Mythopoetic Masculinity and Critique of Traditional, Hegemonic Masculinity*

The men's group participants are clearly involved in constructing a discourse of masculinity in opposition to what they see as the dominant discourse. I now shift to the more immediately personal sides of the discourse in which the men are reconstructing what it means to be a man; they are refiguring their personal identities through this group interaction. This will further develop and add to the findings of the two previous sections. In this section I examine core elements of the positive side of the discourse: creativity, honesty, adventurousness, emotional intimacy, personal growth, and empowerment, among others. These are discussed as often lacking in men's identities and lives in general. New formulations are being constructed for such issues as conflict, anger, and emotional aggression. Personal qualities that are being rejected include "shaming" others and physical aggressiveness. These qualities are seen as integral to the hegemonic discourse of masculinity and are explicitly evaluated as profane and as opposed to the men's groups' alternative discourse.

Creativity, emotional openness, and some sense of freedom are oriented to as central components of the local discourse by all men's group members and are frequently advocated by Watani. During my first meeting with Watani, he praised the children's art school used for meetings as an appropriate location for a men's group. "Isn't it great? It's a good space. They're doing unicorns this week; last week they were doing walruses, the week before, whales [referring to watercolors hung on the wall]. It's so perfect for a men's group. It's so creative, open, free." Expressing one's emotions through creative thinking is continually advocated and pursued. Poetry is a central part of this and of the group context as a whole and it is an integral part of the initiation of new members. Members are welcome to read a poem at any time during the meeting and the person who takes the "speaking stick" home each week is expected to bring a poem in the next week. Almost every member writes their own poetry at least once in a while.

As Watani welcomed me into his group, he encouraged me to get involved in writing poetry. He told me how Robert Bly writes his poetry: "You know, Robert Bly, what he does is he'll just think of a line all of a sudden and it just sounds really good to him; you know, the words just fit together perfectly to say something that really works. And he says, just find a drawer in your house and just use it for this, just write down that line and put it right in the drawer and don't worry about it. And then when you think of another line, whenever, write it down and throw it in there too ... Forcing it just doesn't work."

When I asked group members about why they read and write poetry, they spoke of the power of poetry to help them explore their emotions in ways that might be difficult to do otherwise. Henry said, "I find that sometimes I'll read a poem and it'll really do something to me. It'll bring up things I didn't know were in there. Like recently I was reading this poem and I kind of starting crying.... So I brought it in and it felt great to read it for the group and tell everyone how deeply it touched me." Others expressed very similar feelings. Anthony said, "Poetry gets me right out of 'busy mind,' like worrying about this or that, thinking about what I need to do today, who I need to call and whatever. It takes me to a place where I usually don't go and where it's sometimes just easier not to go there.... It gets me feeling emotions that are really deep and tucked away." In fact, Watani referred to *The Rag and Bone Shop of the Heart,* a collection of poems and stories about men edited by Robert Bly, James Hillman, and Michael Meade (1992), as "the bible of the group." Many members own their own copies of this book and men read poems from it regularly at the beginning of group meetings.

Emotional intimacy is a closely related underlying principle. Sharing personal feelings with others is done through check-ins and through the discussion that makes up the main body of each night's meeting. As has been examined, this definition of the situation is actively maintained by Watani in his efforts to socialize the members. Of course it is also actively maintained by the members themselves. A highly charged incident between David and Talu illustrates this well. This incident started with Talu doing a dramatic, nonverbal check-in: he picked up a maraca to start his check-in, looked at it, and then pounded himself in the chest, head, and stomach with it several times, very hard. Then he turned the handle inward and made a very violent stabbing motion with it into his chest, imitating a suicidal self-stabbing. He then paused and said, "That's it." The next person did his check-in, but during his turn David accused Talu of breaching the code of sharing. "How can you do that?" David challenged Talu, asking him how he can "do this violent bursting-out thing" and then not talk, not "share." Clearly angry, David said he wanted to know "what that's all about." However, nothing more was done about this incident at the time. The men continued going around the circle doing check-ins. Later, Watani opened the floor for anyone who "has something to share" and David instantly jumped on the opportunity, saying that he wanted to hear from Talu, that Talu's earlier act "really pissed me off." David explained that he's just sitting there and then he gets "all this shit dumped on me." He said that he doesn't want to be "dumped on" without an explanation, and so he wanted to hear about what's happening. Talu was then compelled to share, and he finally told the story of the emotionally painful events that had caused the earlier outburst. David had effectively policed the discourse by making Talu maintain the local codes of directness, openness, and intimacy.

Watani argues that some men cannot handle closeness and that sometimes the emotional intensity of the group context frightens them away. "A lot of guys will ... drop out after four weeks or so.... [One example is that] they explode, crying and really getting into it and letting things out, and the guys are saying 'great,' being really supportive and everything, then he's gone the next time. He got too close and opened up too much and then he runs away. Some guys are like that."

One way this principle of closeness is practiced in an embodied way is in the group hug that takes place at the end of each meeting. Watani expressed his pleasure in this: "That's so rare in this culture. What a wonderful thing to have a group of men hugging like that, a group of good men."

As Watani reports, the group context is explicitly meant to be open to spontaneity and to be a place for men to express themselves in whatever ways they want. However, there are still two things that are completely forbidden. As Watani proclaims, "The only rule is no shaming and no physical aggression." Watani explained that "shaming" is something that men's groups in general try to avoid. In fact, in a phone interview I conducted with another local men's group leader, he proclaimed that men are importantly shaped by "shaming" in their lives, for example, the teasing and harassment on the school yard as boys. Another example the leader gave was that of a man being "a bad winner" after beating someone in competition, emphasizing and ridiculing the other man's loss.

The prohibition against shaming is another code that, if violated, will be enforced in the group. This policing is most often done by Watani but also by other members. In this way, the discourse of mythopoetic masculinity is maintained and defended against potential symbolic threats. This is seen in an interesting interaction in which William accused Watani of shaming him. William was able to make Watani back down from an earlier position, in part through this claim that Watani had violated the "no shaming" rule. Before the official start of the group meeting, we were talking about the Halloween party that would take place the following week. Watani, smiling somewhat sarcastically and looking rather mischievously at William, said, "I can't wait to see this guy's costume." Watani appeared to be teasing William, who had expressed resistance to the party. William smiled back, but also looked rather annoyed. He responded with a note of anger in his voice, telling Watani that he felt like Watani was "shaming me into going." William was very adamant about not wanting to be pressured into going through "guilt" and argued that Watani wasn't dealing with him directly and that it should be his choice whether or not to attend the party and how to participate if he did. Watani lost his smile at that point and somewhat deflatedly said that it was fine if William chose not to participate and that of course it's up to everyone how they participate. The issue was not discussed further. Watani, in what he apparently saw originally as a humorous interaction, was called to a kind of impromptu court in front of the whole group. He was charged with violating the "no shaming" law (which is a violation of the larger discourse) that he himself proclaims, and he was compelled to plead guilty.

Conflict and anger are generally regarded by members of men's groups as profane and potentially quite problematic on a practical level. However, conflict and anger are also discussed and actively constructed as tools for further emotional "work," an overarching goal of the movement. Given the discursive emphasis on sensitivity to others, creativity, sharing, not shaming, and closeness, it is not surprising that conflict and anger are ideologically contested terrain. As seen in some exchanges I present here, the men negotiate the place of "niceness" and conflict in group interactions.

In a particularly interesting interaction, Scott, Watani, and David debated the issues of success, closure, and conflict. David and Talu had just been involved in a rather intense exchange in which they seemed to have resolved some important issues. They hugged and there was a pause. Scott broke the silence in a challenging way, suggesting that this had been really good and it seemed like they worked through "some good stuff here," but that he wanted to avoid "some kind of false closure" where people "just make all happy" when that's not really what's going on. Scott is maintaining a major claim that in some sense these two men are pretending to have reached a resolution and that in reality conflict still rages under the surface. Watani responded to this critical challenge by arguing for the concept of a "small closure," a "small victory, a little sixty-watt victory." He said it wasn't "a huge searchlight victory" like at "some Hollywood opening or something" but that nonetheless "it inspires" and then there can be "another sixty-watt victory" and then another and that "that's the way things work."

Watani finds a middle ground between Scott's position and the position that the issue has been completely resolved and there is now a complete lack of conflict. Watani's strategic maneuvering has both maintained his appearance of following the discourse and has reaffirmed the discourse itself. However, David was apparently not completely satisfied that the job of symbolic maintenance had been sufficiently executed. He said that he sometimes gets irritated by the way Scott is "always judging, always prodding....We don't always need to know exactly what you think." There was definitely some real hostility behind this. Scott explained that he was just trying to help bring out issues and that he doesn't mean it in a mean-spirited way. He said he wants the group to be about "exploring" and "opening up" and not about "putting on a happy face" about difficult issues.

This extended interaction exposes the potential contradiction between sensitivity and productive conflict that produces growth. What one man might see as "judging" and "prodding" another may see as "exploring" and "opening up." Thus, the basic structure of the overall discourse is not in question, but the exact meaning of certain aspects of the discourse are open to interpretation. It is to be expected that the men will have recurring conflicts over this contested territory.

Another evocative interaction over the issue of conflict brings out more fully different views on the positive effects of conflict in a men's group. Scott and John had been arguing over a number of weighty personal issues. Watani and John both accused Scott of being insensitive to John's emotional pain. Scott responded in no uncertain terms: he's not going to pretend that he doesn't think the things he does, he's not going to "just sit here and make nice" and pretend that nothing is happening. He said that he won't let anyone tell him what he can and can't say and think and that the group isn't just about being nice. "I'm not gonna silence myself," Scott said.

This impassioned plea draws effectively on the discourse's central codes of freedom from external control, freedom of expression, honesty, and openness. Other members responded in agreement to him. Watani responded by saying that conflict is okay and that men in the group don't have to hide it. George agreed, explaining that he doesn't want to feel that people have to avoid conflict, or that it's "not okay to get angry." He said that people just feel that way sometimes and he doesn't want the group to try to "stifle" that. Tom concurred, suggesting that no one wants the group to turn into "a shouting match" but that "we can be civilly angry at each other," and that that's just a reality that everyone needs to accept.

Watani then took the opportunity to try to lead the group on this issue, explaining that conflict can bring out "truth" and lead to greater sharing. He discussed how this is integral to constructing the "safe space" that is an intimate part of building a community of men. He proclaimed that these qualities (a safe space, a community that supports truth telling) are lacking in the larger culture and that the construction of these is precisely what the men's group is about.

Soon afterward, George built on these sentiments, saying that the good thing about conflict is that it brings out the underlying truth, that the group sees what's not going well for someone when people start getting angry. Then Watani read a passage from the group handbook that is clearly meant to be part of the members' internalization of the larger discourse.

The passage read,

> Conflict in the various stages of a group is to be expected and welcomed. Expected, because it is natural for men who are together to have some creative differences. In fact, these differences are what will keep your group alive and growing. Welcomed, because it can help the men of your group to develop trust for each other and to experience the successful resolution of these differences. It is a demonstration that we can have conflict and still remain in the company of men.... Too often, we men ... [fall into] fearing and distrusting other men. Sometimes we get close enough to somebody to have a "fight," a conflict, and if it doesn't work out quickly, we give up that friend. Too bad, because the possibility for deep friendship was just starting. It seems that sometimes men have to "fight" with each other to get close. The creative resolution of conflict can open the door to intimacy.

After the reading, Watani repeated that the group should welcome conflict and that it can bring the men even closer together.

In interviews, the members supported these ideas. A typical portrayal was that of Terrence: "That's what we're about in this group. We're not going anywhere if we're not going deep and dealing with some difficult shit. And that's gonna be hard work that's gonna stir up some heavy emotions. People are gonna argue; they're gonna yell; they're gonna cry; you name it. If that's not happening regularly then we might as well stop coming to group." Terrence's testimony displays a commitment that has been underlying much of the previous data, that is, a commitment to empowerment. "Personal growth," however each member defines it, is one of the central group goals. Men come to mythopoetic groups to try to become better people and to improve their relationships with their wives or girlfriends, children, other family members, and friends. They come to develop a more satisfying life with respect to their careers, to how they spend their time, and to how they set their priorities in life. All of this suggests a vision of an upward path, a narrative of personal improvement.

The concept of personal growth and empowerment synthesizes much of what has already been displayed in the group interaction data. The men have a central belief in the importance of individuals being motivated in their lives by a creative, adventurous, and exploratory spirit. Men are supposed to be thoughtful and introspective as they form a critical relationship with their own identities. They are to reflect on their lives so that they may discover personal truths and try to find "who they really are." In short, men in the groups are encouraged to pursue a path of personal growth and self-development. While this conceptualization is often left vague and undefined in practice, understanding the discourse of mythopoetic masculinity helps explain this cultural vision. The appendix presents the combined empirical findings that constitute the discourse of mythopoetic masculinity.

## CONCLUSION

I have constructed and deployed a theory of cultural discourse analysis here that allows for the discovery of the discourse of mythopoetic masculinity. Men's group members are animated, inspired, and directed by this discourse at the same time that they construct, debate, contest, and negotiate it. The men constitute the movement with this discourse through their motivation to change themselves on a personal level. They seek to alter their lives by becoming more emotionally open, loving, and supportive while at the same time being self-critical, spontaneous, and adventurous. They make efforts to be closer and more responsive to their partners, children, families, and friends. Members of the mythopoetic men's movement try to break down what they see as hegemonic masculinity within themselves and create a counterhegemonic identity that is an alternative to mainstream practices. While their discourse can be made analytically clear, there are also contradictions, incoherencies, weaknesses, and unfulfilled intentions within that discourse. In vague ways, members of the men's groups seek a world that is more communal and spiritual and that reaches a higher level of freedom, individuality, and justice. Of course this is all focused on the micro level. True to their individualistic ethos, they have no macrolevel political plan for bringing about their goals.

## APPENDIX

### The Discourse of Mythopoetic Masculinity

#### Discursive structure of motives

| *Liberational code* | *Hegemonic code* |
|---|---|
| Faithful | Unfaithful |
| Reliable | Unreliable |
| Personal | Impersonal |
| Attentive | Neglectful |
| Communicative | Quiet/removed |
| Spiritual | Material/atheistic/overly rational |
| Open-minded | Close-minded |
| Relaxed | Uptight |
| Creative | Unimaginative |
| Adventurous/exploratory | Cautious |
| Direct | Oblique |
| Empowered | Disempowered |

#### Discursive structure of social relationships

| *Liberational code* | *Hegemonic code* |
|---|---|
| Emotionally open | Emotionally closed-off |
| Supportive | Disapproving/condemning |
| Trusting | Suspicious |
| Truthful | Deceitful |
| Close/intimate | Distant |
| Loving | Hateful/unloving |
| Respectful | Disrespectful |
| Critical | Deferential |
| Growing | Stagnating |

#### Discursive structure of social institutions

| *Liberational code* | *Hegemonic code* |
|---|---|
| Emotionally safe | Emotionally dangerous |
| Unified | Factional |
| Cooperative/communal | Competitive |
| Sacred | Profane/corrupt |
| Freedom | Control/oppression |
| Spontaneous | Habitual |
| Individuality | Conformity |
| Justice | Injustice |

## NOTES

1. For a detailed analysis of the history of cultural thought, see Alexander and Smith (1993).

2. This avoids the "cultural dope" problem identified most prominently by Garfinkel (1967). See also Wrong (1961). Actors must be seen as *both* constituted by culture and able to change it. Thus, culture is both internal and external to any individual actor. It unconsciously guides action at the same time that it can be picked apart, criticized, debated, negotiated, and changed.

3. Individuals and institutions do not have to be explicitly allied with the mythopoetic men's movement to be evaluated as positive according to the discourse of mythopoetic masculinity. Nor do they even have to self-identify as having a counterhegemonic identity. Correspondingly, self-professed members or institutions of the mythopoetic men's movement can be criticized as embodying in certain ways the hegemonic codes.

4. There is clearly a cultural tension here that is both potentially disruptive and potentially productive. Emotional safety and supportiveness are central codes at the same time that constructive criticism is valued as well. It is a matter of opinion in any given case what the difference is between a helpful piece of advice and an attack, between a supportive suggestion and a mean-spirited insult. This is an inevitable outcome of the logic of this discourse.

5. See Willis (1977) and Hebdige (1979) for interesting analyses of not fully articulated critiques of hegemonic culture. This is close to what I am discussing here, although I am not using a traditional Marxist framework. I have chosen to orient my analysis more closely to the members' meanings themselves, rather than impose a model of "correct" criticism on them. That is to say, Marxist work has a tendency to hold over actors a model of what "full" realization of oppression looks like and then accuse almost everyone of not being perceptive enough to reach that standard. Related to this, see Fantasia (1988) for a discussion of how social analysts have consistently assumed that actors need to have a "fully developed" critique of the social world before they can act to change it. Rather, it is important to appreciate the partial, changing, and often internally contradictory nature of concrete, individual ideological belief.

6. I explore this interesting symbolic conflict more in chapter 5. This is a major site of internal conflict within the group: the belief by some that (a) there is a clear dichotomy between personal and political and (b) the work in this group must be solely personal. Of course this flies in the face of the history of women's feminist consciousness-raising groups, in which the exploding of this binary vision was central.

# The Mythopoetic Ethic and the Spirit of Capitalism

As chapters 2, 3, and 4 have suggested indirectly, the vision of social change of the mythopoetic men's movement goes beyond a simple critique of masculinity. While it is largely untheorized, the critical project of the movement participants involves a significant critique of American culture vis-à-vis the sphere of work and economics. Proceeding inductively for each topic, I first examine what the data show that the men themselves are orienting toward and then progressively analyze the data sociologically to create an analytically coherent, structured understanding of these empirical findings. The second section of the chapter then shows how this critical cultural construction is used concretely to create real changes in the men's lives as well as changes in the lives of their partners, children, other family members, coworkers, and friends.

One of my key findings is that this social critique, while strongly and repeatedly expressed, is ultimately rendered by the men in a disjointed and fractured way. It is conceptualized within a framework of individualism; that is, observations are filtered through direct personal experience and are rarely constructed into a thorough critique of the object of focus. This results in a critical worldview that upon close analysis has clear gaps, contradictions, and omissions, falling far short of what social analysts would identify as a well-developed, systematic critique. Still, the goal of my analysis is not primarily to criticize the mythopoetic men's movement's conceptualization but, rather, to understand it in all its complexity and see how it motivates and changes members' social behavior outside of the mythopoetic context. My ultimate conclusions will be faithful to the members' meanings while at the same time offering a deeper understanding of the social dynamics at play.

The data suggest a complex critical construct concerning what the men conceive of as the dominant culture at this point in history in the United States. Specifically, the men consistently develop a critique of what can be understood as the internalization of an American work ethic. They see themselves as dupes of a dominant cultural belief in the primacy of work, professional achievement, and material success. They sometimes conceptualize this through the popular concept of "workaholism." Moreover, they see the social processes related to the dominant work ethic as dividing people, creating emotional distance that damages the entire society. While this is generally expressed as a microsocial dynamic, it is sometimes brought to the macro level, making it clear that this is not only a social-psychological critique but also a larger, cultural one.

One aspect of this vision is a criticism of rationalization, disenchantment, and a general lack of spiritual fulfillment and love in American society. As I showed in chapter 4, the men often speak of American society as overly regimented, overly focused on efficiency and production, and generally lacking a full sense of spiritual passion and love. This is clearly a grand critique of Western culture that, while not robustly theorized, is a recurrent and strongly expressed moral belief.

After exploring this critical vision in depth, I devote the rest of this chapter to exploring how this moral construct appears to motivate and direct these actors' behavior outside of the context of the men's movement. I show that these cultural ideals are far from limited in their causality to the ideational realm. The ethnographic data in this study span eight years, allowing a longitudinal analysis of change and causality that is rare for ethnography. What the data in fact suggest is the extent to which the guiding ideas developed in the movement have slowly yet pervasively changed the lives of not only the participants themselves but also those with whom the men associate outside of the movement. It is crucial to understand that after constructing and elaborating these ideological conceptualizations, the men take them out into the broader society and affect the social experience of countless people who are not members of the movement. It is in this way that the movement has limited, yet concrete, effects on social reality and is part of the larger historical dynamics of social change occurring in American society.

Previous research on the mythopoetic movement has not seriously examined this issue. There are two main reasons for this. First, when looking at political/cultural issues, earlier work focused almost exclusively on the gender issues involved in the movement. However, while this is a men's movement, it is about more than men and gender. Connections between masculinity and work have been studied elsewhere, but they have not been taken up in a major way with respect to the mythopoetic men's movement. In most previous work, the main goal has been to criticize the movement's gender ideology as being too conservative, thereby missing the ways in which participants are involved in an unusual counterhegemonic project having to do work and economics. The second main reason that this issue has been largely overlooked is methodological. As I discussed in earlier chapters, previous scholarship has almost entirely relied on a content analysis approach, analyzing the written works of movement high intellectuals. Since these political and cultural issues are not covered in a major way in movement texts, they are easily missed. However, my participant observation and interviews uncovered this pattern of thought and behavior on the part of the grassroots participants. They have innovated in the area of political and cultural change largely separate from the leading written works of the movement. This was an entirely inductive discovery that occurred well into the timeline of the research project, the kind of unexpected finding that ethnography is so effective at generating.

## THE CONSTRUCTION AND CRITIQUE OF THE AMERICAN WORK ETHIC

The members of the mythopoetic men's movement consistently criticize what they identify as a core cultural belief in the central importance of work and professional achievement. However, this is not a detached analysis; rather, they speak of how they have unwittingly internalized this belief to the point that they themselves are some of its most extreme adherents. This is an interesting and subtle criticism that further elucidates their conceptualization of the idea of cultural hegemony (as discussed in chapter 4).

A vast majority of the men I studied stated at one time or another that some kind of work ethic is one of the defining characteristics of their lives. For the most part, the men clearly identify this as a problem in their lives that they want to solve through participation in the movement. This understanding of the nature of modern life appears to correspond with parts of Max Weber's cultural theory of capitalism presented in *The Protestant Ethic and the Spirit of Capitalism* (Weber 1992). The relevant part of Weber's argument is that capitalism can be understood as a moral order, a secular morality that emphasizes the fundamental goodness of hard work and material production. Under this cultural system, it becomes a virtue to be a successful capitalist. In terms of the cultural discourse theory of chapter 4 of this book, hard work becomes a sacred code, a foundational good that is to a certain extent an end in and of itself. (It should be noted that Weber refers to a period of history immediately preceding modern capitalism when discussing the spirit of capitalism.)

It is this secular work ethic that the men identify and criticize. This is almost always done on an individualistic level and is rarely explicitly generalized to a macrocultural order. Nonetheless, these men are reporting what one would expect them to report under a cultural system of this kind: they repeatedly cite a compulsion to work and to be productive in the material sphere. Alex made this clear in an interview: "I guess it's just what I do. I mean, when I grew up, my parents taught me to work hard and do well in school. They put a lot of pressure on me and it sure worked. I did great in school and it really paid off. Now I still work hard and I've got a great business to show for it. It's just that I'm beginning to wonder if it's all worth it." During a group meeting, Anthony explained his experience of this dynamic very clearly, complaining about how unfulfilling it is and saying that he is "just locked into it" and that it is "automatic." He explained that "I don't even connect it to any ends anymore," that it is just "compulsive." Anthony called himself a "workaholic." Mario echoed this sentiment: "It's like I don't even think about it. I just get up in the morning and do the routine: brush my teeth, shower, have breakfast, go to work, then come home and go to sleep. I mean, I like my work but is it worth it to just be so robotic about it and make that my whole life? I heard in Japan they have a name for it: 'salaryman,' businessmen who just ... that's all they do is work."

A majority of the men in the movement are successful members of the hardworking middle class, upper middle class, or upper class. They have been driven to succeed their entire lives and generally hold positions of prestige and power. They uniformly identify themselves as having believed in hard work and material success. However, they have begun to question these cultural values and this lifestyle, which has become for them "compulsive" and "robotic." These men feel that they are enacting a social script that may not actually be serving their larger interests, and they are critically examining the worth of a devotion to work that eclipses other aspects of their lives. They wonder whether it is "all worth it," whether they should make work their whole lives.

This critique has a social-psychological, individualistic basis. The men are asking themselves whether their devotion to material success is actually in their best interests. These are men who have largely succeeded in the economic realm of American society, accumulating material resources and establishing prestigious careers. At this point in their lives, they are reporting that this success has not led to their happiness and that they are still unsatisfied in their lives. However, it is not simply that they are missing some other things in their lives that they would like to add to their existing professional lives; they are specifically identifying what they see as the negative necessary outcome of this work ethic.[1]

The members of the men's groups complain of "emptiness" that they feel in their lives due to their focus on work. Anthony explained this feeling one night in a group meeting after returning from a vacation. He said that his week of vacation had been great but now that he's "back in the groove," he doesn't want to be there. He said that the "pressure and expectations leave me empty," that he has to "give away all of myself" because he is constantly "performing" and "taking care of things." Anthony's work as a high-powered lawyer often leaves him feeling "bored," wondering "what's the point," like he's on a "treadmill," and he said that he wonders "what is it all for?" and that it "all seems kind of silly and empty."

Kevin built on this typical sentiment by explaining how unfulfilling his life is despite his professional success. He said that he feels a "void," or "emptiness" that he has trouble putting into words. He didn't know why he feels this way, given that he has a successful career, a "good amount of money" in the bank, free time, a nice house, and a nice car. He felt "kind of embarrassed" about it, because he "has no excuse to feel this way" since he's "so fortunate in so many ways." Kevin said he's been feeling this way for the past few years and wants to somehow find his way out of this situation.

Kevin is typical in identifying this problem but not having a ready solution. Many men have trouble conceptualizing these issues. They are aware of these feelings of emptiness, lack of fulfillment, and frustration. They connect these feelings to what is missing in a life focused on work and professional achievement, but they struggle to make sense of the paradox that they have "made it" according to mainstream notions of success but are still unsatisfied. Kevin is even embarrassed about it. He lacks the cultural resources to explain his situation, so much so that he feels guilty for being dissatisfied. The men are at a liminal point culturally; they have spent their lives achieving what they have been told will make them happy, fulfilled people and now that they have arrived, they are beginning to think the whole plan might have been flawed from the beginning.

An exchange between Sam and Anthony shows an interest in a work experience that is worthwhile beyond merely providing a paycheck. Anthony explained that after twenty-four years of being a lawyer, he's not sure he wants to do it any more. He's simply "not getting much out of it." It's just a job that pays the bills and supports his family, "thank God," but that's all it is. Sam agreed, saying that you can have your own company, the investments, the prestige, the house and a lot of "stuff," but "what does is mean?" He asked the group, "Doesn't it all seem kind of empty?" Anthony responded that he wants something more, that he wants to feel like he's doing something worthwhile, something where he's contributing to the world in a real way and people appreciate that he's doing something significant that makes a difference.

These men want success and they want to be able to support their families, but they want more than this traditional life path offers. Their critique of the life of striving for material success goes beyond simply identifying that it lacks meaning, doesn't offer fulfillment, or is not worthwhile. In fact, they develop a fairly sophisticated criticism of the emotional unhealthiness of this culturally proscribed lifestyle. Again, it is a critique based on individualistic, social-psychological thinking. Nonetheless, they are clearly making larger claims about their culture.

One of the men's critical points about the emotional damage caused by participation in this traditional model of work is based on claims concerning stress, pressure, and anxiety. This is a repeated topic in group discussions. For instance, Alex said that he constantly feels in "fight or flight mode" because of work, traffic, noise, and "the constant hustle and bustle" of getting everything done. He said it's "constant adrenaline," constant stress, a constant "state of crisis." It all leads to "sickness, trouble, and meltdown," he declared. "We're not built for that." There is an indication here of serious emotional difficulties; Alex wasn't just complaining about being a little overworked but referring to what appears to be a serious issue in his life. He makes references to emotional overload and potential psychological breakdown.

John made a similar point, underscoring the sense of constant anxiety and stress that these men report experiencing. John wanted to get "his priorities straight." Work takes up too much of his life, he said. It's a constant state of activity, of "frenzy," always moving, always getting things done, "being productive." Carl agreed, saying it's like "always being on a tightrope." The tightrope imagery evokes well the sense of second-to-second pressure that the men report experiencing.

They feel that they have to be completely focused and never make a mistake or they will plummet to their metaphorical deaths.

Henry described what he calls "the Wall." He evoked with lucidity the feeling of being completely overwhelmed that these men seem to experience regularly. He said he often hits "the Wall" from long periods of stress and exhaustion, and then he has to "collapse" at the end of the day and simply has no energy for anything else. All he can handle is "zoning out" in front of the TV in order to relax before bed.

Nick drew a striking picture of the feeling of being consumed by work and how it damages his entire life. He explained that he "feels compelled to keep busy" because of his "work ethic." He finds it hard to relax. Because he owns his own business, he feels a constant need to work, to monitor, to check and stay on top of things. He said that he feels "so sucked in" to everything and everybody related to work that he can't really relax in the city, that he needs to get out of town to really feel free, away from telephones, pagers, faxes, and so on. This man is trapped in this state whenever he is in his own home city. During the vast majority of his life, even while in his own home, he is compelled to follow the dictates of this work ethic. Using the Weberian notion of the iron cage, Nick can be seen as a captive in this cage of the work ethic, of modern rationalization. It is a cage built out of the socially constructed need for productivity, efficiency, and success. Technology plays a part in this: telephones, pagers, and faxes and the nonstop connectivity they bring are all part of this iron cage.

The men designate these experiences *dysfunctional,* drawing from the terminology of recovery groups and pop psychology. They often refer to their lives as being dysfunctionally devoted to work or to their having a "dysfunctional relationship to" their careers. As previous research has identified (Schwalbe 1996), this conceptual framework is drawn in part from Alcoholics Anonymous. The notion of "workaholism" that the men I studied use frequently is clearly consistent with this general milieu. Mario used these terms to support Nick's earlier point about how work colonizes the rest of his life. He declared in a self-deprecating tone that at least some people are "functional workaholics" but that he's a "dysfunctional workaholic." He declared that the rest of his life is not working because of his work "addiction."

The men in the movement develop a fairly sophisticated conceptualization of the social psychology of what they are constructing as the achievement ideology of modern America. They see themselves as actors playing out the script of modern culture. However, the complexity of their conceptualization is in the way that they see themselves as emotionally complicit in the maintenance of the system. They see themselves as having internalized these ideals to the point that they enact them out of a sense of immediate, personal, emotional need.[2]

One way that the men conceptualize their participation in this cultural work ethic is through a personal drive to achieve at ever-increasing levels. The process is an infinite one because there is no actual end point. Watani invented the term *not-enough mind,* innovated from the Buddhist idea of different kinds of mind. The term caught on in his groups and has become a repeated resource for the expression of this idea. One of his first uses of this term came when the men were discussing having "pathologically high standards" in their work lives. David said his glass is half empty because his glass in too big.... Sam said he's always unsatisfied, that he always wants more. Watani jumped in and said that what everyone was talking about is "not-enough mind," that we have been trained to think that we never have enough and that we have to keep on working for more and more. Gary, Nick, David, Terrence, Henry, and Dana all agreed verbally in various ways, particularly in terms of the issues of money and career. The men seemed happy to have a term to describe this condition.

The men connect the need to achieve constantly in the material realm with the need to feel good about themselves as men. Andrew clearly elaborated this conceptualization, declaring that masculinity "is all about achievement." For instance, he said, being a CEO is like being the captain of a ship, a leader above everyone. (Andrew has experience as the CEO of a major corporation.) It's about taking on responsibility and not accepting help, he said, because you're a man and you don't need it. He explained that his childhood was defined by this drive for achievement, that he had to be smart to prove himself to his parents and to the world. He learned to achieve in order to show worth and to not complain about anything but keep on going. These concepts correspond directly to the construction of hegemonic masculinity discussed in depth in chapter 4.[3]

The men connect this culturally proscribed, internalized need for achievement to combating feelings of lack of worth, low self-image, and fear of failure. They describe situations in which they feel that they must always prove themselves and always make it clear to themselves and everyone else that they are "good people." The men suggest that the primary way (or one of the primary ways) they have to do this is through professional achievement. In a significant exchange, the men developed a social-psychological analysis of the connection between identity, emotional needs, and the work ethic they had been discussing. First they began by identifying the general problem: during check-ins, four men brought up work issues in a critical light. Andrew said that he's taking six business trips around the United States and to Australia in the next few weeks and that he feels like he's constantly trying to get things done to get to the next thing. It's not that he's necessarily unhappy about what he's doing, he explained, it's just that he wants to do it "at a healthy pace," "in a sane way." He wants a chance to "live life," "to be present and aware" instead of "fanatically" rushing from task to task. Mario checked in next and agreed with Andrew's general point. He said business is a "constant struggle" and that he never has time "to really take care of things." Sam agreed with both of them about work issues and said that he always feels a "compulsion" to be getting things done, to be crossing things off the lists that he's always making. Dana said he feels overwhelmed a lot and realizes that he often checks in saying he has "too many balls in the air."

For the men's check-ins to be so thematically focused around one issue without any provocation is a notable event in the group. Dana pointed this out after the check-in process concluded, and the men then engaged in a revealing discussion about these issues, constructing a social-psychological vision of the ways that the work ethic functions on an emotional level. Dana took the stick and said that it seemed like it's something "that's really happening for people." Nick responded that he really has a problem with this, that he always works hard even when it's not that necessary. He doesn't really understand it but wants to change, to get more "healthy and balanced" about it. Mario agreed, saying he feels "this huge pressure" to always be getting things done. He feels like he needs to "justify himself," to show that he's doing a good job, that he's "worthwhile." Several men signal their agreement. Mario continued by saying that he always feels like maybe he's "not good enough." Nick supported and further developed this idea, saying that "it's definitely about fear for me, ... fear of failure, ... fear that I'm going to fuck it up" and let people down and that people will then think less of him. He feels like he has to stay "on top of everything" all the time to avoid this.

Mario is constructing an explanatory system in which the drive to achieve in the professional realm is driven by a need to prove himself, to show that he is a "worthwhile" individual. The men are exposing a deep-seated anxiety and fear of failure that they report keeps them strongly participating in this cultural milieu of the work ethic. It appears that the motivation is not simply an internalization of a positive valence attached to hard work, which is certainly part of the cultural dynamic. Instead, it seems that at a deeper level, the motivation is also one of an almost desperate avoidance of a deeply profane evaluation: that of a failed person, a man who has been unable to live up to the minimum standards of human worthiness.

Henry followed Nick, agreeing with him and adding another dimension to the conceptualization. He said that it's also about "hiding out" for him. If he stays busy, he pointed out, then he doesn't have to face other things in life, he doesn't have to face his real feelings and other difficult emotional things. Henry said that his father was always like that and he learned it from him. Sam agreed with Henry's characterization of work as a method of avoidance. In this way, he said, "we don't have to face ourselves." If we keep a "constant racket of chaos" and activity, he reasoned, then there's no time "to see yourself" and to have to see your emotions and your pain. He said that as soon as he finishes one thing, then it's immediately on to the next thing, with no time for reflection.

Watani stepped in to further shape this cultural construction that the group is creating. He asked the group to think about the question "Who am I trying to please?" He suggested that maybe it's their fathers, mothers, girlfriends or wives, or perhaps other guys and coworkers. "Ask yourself why you're doing it and does it make sense." The group continued the discussion, further elaborating this conceptual scheme. David indicated his strong agreement with the point about work as avoidance. Someone made a point about compulsive work being a "dysfunctional obsession" and the group executed a loud "aho" in agreement.

In this interaction and many others like it, group members construct a critical characterization of what can be understood as a typical lifestyle of hardworking, successful (disproportionately male) professionals. They are criticizing the dominant culture, saying that they have internalized certain cultural values that drive them into what they see as an emotionally unhealthy existence.

Certainly the men's critical focus is individualistic and personal. They are interested in how they feel and what negative effects are happening to them. They are not primarily concerned with the effects on others, except in the case of others in the same situation as them. They are also not concerned with constructing a careful macrosystemic theory about how these dynamics work on a broader societal level. Thus, there is the temptation to criticize the incompleteness of their theorization as well as the strongly social-psychological, personal, and even self-serving nature of their critique. Nonetheless, it is clear that the men are developing a surprisingly critical characterization of a cultural system of which they have, on the surface, been the direct beneficiaries. They have obtained the prestige, authority, and material resources that are valued in modern society and yet they turn around and indict the very foundation of that success, the work ethic that created it. Although only a partial critique, this is certainly a major break from acceptance of what they see as the larger cultural system that constrains them.

Another aspect of the men's criticism of the modern work ethic is the argument that the striving for success has no end, that there is no final resting point after victory. The men paint it as a never-ending quest in which actual satisfaction is elusive or impossible. In a specific, detailed explanation during a group meeting, Nick portrayed his experience of this dynamic. He discussed his feelings about running the construction business of which he is the sole owner. Nick said that "they keep moving the goal posts another ten yards." You're finally getting close, he explained, then "God yanks out the rug and laughs at you." He explained that his business had been quite successful and that he had been trying to get to the point where he can clear out all his company's debt, build the business to a certain point, and then "start making some real money." He had been building debt for the past four years when business had been a little slow, but he had been paying it back as well. Nick said he keeps thinking he has about six months to "finally hit the sweet spot" and "step up to a new level," but that goal keeps getting pushed back. He said that he keeps "reaching for the brass ring" and then "it gets yanked away" and explained that financial issues keep standing in his way and negating his progress. For instance, he'll "get sued or get screwed on some house from two years ago" because a contractor he hired did a poor job on something and has now gone out of business and disappeared. So Nick has to submit the claim to his insurance company and "take a big hit later" or fix the problem himself out of pocket now and save money in the long run. He said he does it himself, but it sets him back and that "this kind of thing just keeps happening." You get "paranoid" after a while, he said, so that if things are going well, you're always looking over your shoulder, waiting for the other shoe to drop: a letter from the IRS, a call from a lawyer, or something similar.

This lengthy exchange shows in a distinct and precise way the extent of frustration and fear that can eat away at the consciousness of even the most successful businessman. He clearly desires material achievement but it constantly eludes him, creating deep and pervasive emotional difficulties. He perpetually experiences the paranoia and fear of impending doom despite the surface appearances of success. These revealing ethnographic data suggest the possible underbelly of economic attainment in modern life. Later, Nick explained that this is a very common phenomenon among businessmen. He said that he's seen it over and over again with people he knows. "They're making more money than I'll ever make; they've got it all, the houses, the cars, the yachts, whatever" and yet they keep working. In fact, he explained, they're even more driven than he is. "They love it. It's a big game for them. They live for it." He explained that these overachieving businessmen are consumed by this need to succeed, and they never rest. "They keep working 'til they drop dead, and what do they really have to show for it?"

Mario, who partially owns a four-star hotel, runs a hotel management company, and is a successful real estate investor, responded to Nick's point and underscored the perpetual fear and emotional instability that this life involves. He confirmed this feeling of the goalposts always moving further and further so you can never reach them. He said it's just part of life and that you can always "lose everything tomorrow." Mario discussed the anxiety of constantly preparing, worrying, and trying to avoid financial disaster.

Thus far in this chapter, my analysis has identified a distinct and particular critique of the culture of the American work ethic. The men of the mythopoetic men's movement have constructed a critical understanding of the emotional downside of the traditional model of the financially successful worker. They are creating an unusual understanding of the experience they take to be common for successful mainstream businessmen. They are beginning to wonder if the cultural agenda they have been taught is fundamentally wrong in certain ways.

This dynamic of questioning traditional goals presents a real puzzle for these men and, as such, they often have difficulty conceptualizing the problem. It would appear that they are criticizing a foundational ethos of their culture. As such, it is not an easy process, as they are in a liminal cultural moment. They clearly have some rudimentary tools to criticize the dominant culture, yet they are also at a loss to fully conceptualize their dawning critique. They respond to the situation by innovating, by developing new cultural understandings of the experiences of their lives. As discussed earlier in the chapter, it is an unusual historical situation: they are the apparent beneficiaries of their culture's economic arrangements and yet they persist in laboring over new critical conceptualizations. Their critique is not founded on claims of exclusion based on class, race and ethnicity, gender, sexual orientation, or any other marker of identity. The fascinating dynamic is that they have all the indicators of success yet they still insist on developing a cultural and social-psychological critique of American society.

This is an unusual development: a critique of modern society from the top, not premised on the desire for inclusion and economic success for their identity group. It is an internal critique, based not on theories of social justice for the excluded, such as Marxist or socialist thought, racial justice theories, feminism, or gay and lesbian liberation theory. Rather, it attacks modern society on a different level, suggesting that success in traditional mainstream material terms may not even be worth attaining in the first place. Perhaps in this sense it is not a liberal critique but a radical one, one that questions a fundamental, foundational belief of modern Western culture. Still, it is clear that these men are not specifically bent on dramatically altering society in a systematic, structural way. True to their individualistic ethos, they seek local, private solutions that will address perceived problems at a social-psychological level.[4] The rest of this chapter addresses the question of how they are mobilizing to change the circumstances of their lives to address what they have constructed as the problems inherent in the project of mainstream economic success.

## INSTITUTIONALIZING ALTERNATIVES TO THE MODEL OF MAINSTREAM MATERIAL SUCCESS

A major focus of the mythopoetic men's movement is inspiring men to create change in their lives. The groups are far more than mere discussion groups. The ideas developed within the groups, at campouts, and during workshops and retreats are meant to be put directly into service in the men's lives as they see fit. No specific change is encouraged; men bring up issues and problems in their lives during open-ended interactions and are then expected to address those issues outside of the mythopoetic context. This is meant to be unique to each man; specific actions are determined by him based in part on ongoing discussion, advice, and guidance from fellow members.

There will be concrete effects both inside and outside the movement based on how the men frame certain issues, what cultural values they develop, and what kinds of discourses they construct. As I show later in the chapter, ideas developed over time in the mythopoetic context are turned into concrete action in the lived world outside of the movement framework. That is to say, the cultural constructs developed interactively have real causal power; they are mobilized in ways that literally change these men's lives. They do not simply affect the way the men think but directly effect the ways they act in society.

In fact, ideas change not only the lives of the men themselves but also by extension the lives of many who are part of the men's interactive circles. Concrete effects are seen in the lives of wives, girlfriends, mothers and fathers, brothers and sisters, sons and daughters, friends, coworkers, casual acquaintances, and more. Many of the people who are affected have little or no understanding of the mythopoetic men's movement and may well be unaware that the changes have stemmed from the movement in the first place. Indeed, it is impossible to calculate the enormous number of people who have been affected in some way or another by more than one hundred thousand of these men. Perhaps many of those affected have never even heard of the movement, but in some way their lives have been different because of it.

The evidence of these changes outside of the movement context are reported, not directly observed. Given the methodological approach of this study, it is not feasible to observe men in their lives and have systematic firsthand evidence of these developments. Suffice it to say, however, that the reported dynamics discussed in this section have been discussed on multiple occasions within the context of the deep, intimate, and confidential setting of the men's group context. All of the findings here have also been supported by in-depth, open-ended interview data on separate occasions. For the sake of brevity and readability, only a fraction of the supporting data available actually appears here in print.

One of the central tenets of "men's work," as the members would say, is to use the lessons learned inside the movement to improve one's life. The men's work is explicitly conceived of as an ongoing cyclical process of interaction between mythopoetic activity and the outside social world. Issues from men's lives are raised in a mythopoetic context and discussed at length; ideas and new insights are developed and taken out into "the real world"; changes are made and the changes are then discussed in the mythopoetic context; and the process begins again. There can be any number of iterations of this process. Indeed, I observed many specific topics for particular men traverse this cyclical process countless times for years at a stretch during my research.

An emphasis on creating change is a central part of Watani's socializing agenda. He told me this clearly when I was entering his group.

> You know, on one hand, these are discussion groups. The majority of what we do is talk. But don't let that fool you. What we're really doing is growing and addressing our issues, you know, becoming more mature, wise, and loving men. If this group isn't making your life better, then you need to reexamine what you're doing here. Either you're perfect ... [smiles] or you're holding back and not really doing the work. It's not easy. It would be a lot easier to stay at home and watch TV, just stay the same old, mainstream person, wallowing in this dead culture. It's your choice. Every man has to make that commitment or a group isn't going to work.

During one group meeting, Watani reminded the men of this idea in a different way, saying that the group shouldn't "coddle fragility," that each man should "own your group" and be fully "present and responsible" for making it work for him and his life. He said that everyone needs to have a "contract" to make it work, both inside and outside the group. This group, Watani explained, is not about "whining" but about "doing." Watani is also fond of "quoting" the "great Zen master Nike Roshi" as saying "Just Do It" (referring to the Nike sportswear advertising slogan). He uses this verbal tactic regularly to encourage the men to stop talking, delaying, or avoiding and start creating real change in their lives.[5]

Members of the men's groups regularly remind each other of this expectation of action in the world. One night during a group meeting, Ken introduced the concept of "telling your story for the last time," an interesting resource for encouraging change. Ken explained that he recently attended a talk by a well-known Buddhist teacher, Catherine Ingram, and said that he really liked her discussion about "telling your story for the last time." He explained that throughout your life you get out your story so many times and in so many ways and that over time as you work on your "issues" you begin to resolve them and your old story begins to melt away because it is no longer relevant. Eventually, then, you tell your story for the last time. People responded positively to this idea, and Watani clearly agreed with it very strongly, suggesting that "Maybe some of you will tell your own stories for the last time right here in this group." Ken then explained how tired he is of his story of work and money and of never having enough satisfaction with either and how he desperately wants to "get beyond" that. This concept of telling one's story for the last time was integrated into the group discourse and used off and on for years afterward.

The men's focus on the American work ethic is a major target of this agenda of individualistic social change. As shown earlier in this chapter, the men regularly criticize what they identify as an unhealthy and unjust social pressure toward material achievement and professional success. However, following the focus on concrete change, this critical treatment is not allowed to be simply an occasion to "let off steam" for the men. While they certainly see themselves as addressing the symptoms of social problems, they also emphasize addressing the causes of those symptoms and solving the problem at the root.

This commitment to creating change in their professional and economic lives is so strong that in many instances the men are not allowed to frame themselves as trapped in a work-related situation. Under certain circumstances, it is a breach of a core belief if a man suggests that he is powerless to create change in his professional life. In the following exchange, Kevin is challenged on these terms. Kevin was complaining about his work and seemed very demoralized by it. Dana stepped in and challenged Kevin by saying that it sounded like he is giving up, that he thinks it's all "fated to happen this way." Dana suggested that maybe there are things Kevin can do to change these things, that maybe he's in a line of work that has difficult aspects to it, but it's not "written in stone" that it has to be going the way it is. Kevin tried to argue that there's nothing he can do about a lot of the things he had been talking about. Several of the men launched into him, suggesting ways he could make changes and criticizing him for being overly "fatalistic" and "defeatist." Gabriel suggested that these problems are probably affecting "his happiness" and "his consciousness" and the rest of his life more than he wants to admit. In the end Kevin seemed to agree and said that he would try out some of the suggestions and tell us in a few weeks how it's going.

On another occasion, the men further police this rule of not conceptualizing oneself as unable to create change related to work issues. Nick was discussing his "love/hate" relationship with work, saying that his business had been very successful but also takes a "huge toll" on him. He said that he was feeling "trapped" in his job and he didn't know what to do about it. Members of the group immediately criticized this conceptualization, arguing that Nick is not really trapped, that "you make your own situation" and that "you trap yourself." Someone argued that you make these choices yourself and you can get out of them yourself too.

Watani emphasized this belief by suggesting a mental exercise designed to encourage the men to reconceptualize their life goals in ways that avoid the lure of material success. He asked, if ten million dollars dropped in your lap, how would you do things differently? Watani said this would be a good exercise for everyone to do for themselves at some point. Design your life around what you really want, he argued, not around "mantras of being trapped."

Watani is trying to induce the men to suspend their internalized belief in financial achievement in order to frame their lives in different terms. He is furthering the group ethos that financial goals should not overly determine the character of one's life. Clearly ten million dollars is not going to drop in each man's lap, but the mental exercise is designed to help the men figure out what they are feeling is missing in their lives, perhaps due to the intensity of their focus on material success. Watani uses the Buddhist term *mantra,* referring to a declaration of belief that is stated repetitively in Buddhist practice to remind oneself of a piece of wisdom or truth. Here he wants the men to conceptualize their feelings of being trapped as merely the product of unreflective beliefs that they repeat to themselves in a meaningless, rote way, resulting in stagnation and unhappiness.

This belief in dynamic change with respect to material issues is a concerted, proactive one. The men talk repeatedly about being the "architects" of their own lives. As discussed earlier in this chapter, the majority of men are in positions of at least reasonable financial success; this attitude toward change can and does produce results for them. They clearly have the ability to carry out this ethos of individual social change and, as shown later in this chapter, they often use this ability effectively.

Everyone in the population sample of this study who was a full participant in the mythopoetic movement for longer than two months reported making at least some significant changes with respect to these issues of changing certain life goals and values. For the long-term participants, their personal growth and ensuing life changes are seen as one and the same as the movement. Indeed, this is a significant part of why they are in the movement in the first place.

The rest of this chapter is devoted to exploring in detail how these men have made specific changes outside of the mythopoetic context in an effort to combat what they have constructed as the generalized cultural belief in a destructive work ethic, unnecessary material accumulation, and unending professional achievement.

There are two major categories of approaches group members have taken to creating change in their lives in these terms. One approach is to dramatically alter one's career path; the other is to make more moderate changes within one's existing career and lifestyle. Examining the longitudinal ethnographic data closely, it is possible to see the life changes as they occur over relatively long periods of time, in most cases several years. My analysis focuses on one member at a time to show the individual changes in a series of case studies.

The first category is composed of the men who have made dramatic, life-altering changes in their professional lives as a result of the cultural discourses developed during their participation in the mythopoetic men's movement. The men in this category have in various ways started their lives on the traditional path of professional and material achievement and have then removed themselves from this social trajectory due to ideas developed in the movement. In order to develop significant depth in individual cases, my analysis focuses on six men in this category: Anthony, Sam, Terrence, Kevin, Andrew, and Dennis. In every case, these men decided to give up a certain amount of financial and professional success in order to achieve what they see as higher goals of a more emotional, spiritual, and personal nature.

The second category of change patterns is composed of men who have decided to maintain their current careers but make changes within them in order to avoid what they see as the destructive effects of an overemphasis on the material realm. Many men fall into this category, but in order to maintain a concise argument, my analysis focuses closely on three men who typify this approach in instructively different ways: David, Nick, and Henry.

## DRAMATIC LIFE CHANGE USING MOVEMENT BELIEFS

Spending time with the men in the movement reveals many stories of men who have been very successful businessmen, lawyers, doctors, and other highly paid professionals and who have decided to change their careers in midlife due to inspiration from the movement. The present analysis focuses on six of these men, each observed over a number of years in multiple contexts of the movement. They are Anthony, Sam, Terrence, Kevin, Andrew, and Dennis.

Anthony began in the mythopoetic movement in the mid-1980s, well before the movement emerged onto the national stage. During the research timeframe, he decided to give up his highly successful law practice as a principled decision that grew directly out of the movement. He had grown tired of working sixty, seventy, and even eighty hours a week in a grueling career that supplied him with plenty of financial resources but little else. During his time in the movement, Anthony developed a different conception of what he wanted his life to be, and his current career did not match that. In the end he decided to drop out of his career to focus his life more on his family and his own personal development.

When Anthony entered the ethnographic sample, he had been practicing law for twenty-one years and had had his own successful private law practice for most of that time. He lived in an extremely exclusive neighborhood, owned a large house and two luxury automobiles, and did not want for material items. He had a well-established family composed of himself, his wife, and their eleven-year-old daughter.

From the beginning, Anthony complained frequently at group meetings about his work life and its effects on the rest of his life. A routine topic of his check-ins was how difficult a day he had just had, how exhausted he was, and how "stressed out" he was from work. For the next few years in group discussions, he regularly discussed how little satisfaction he was getting out of his work and how much of it was mere drudgery, repetitive and unrewarding.

Anthony also complained of how much his work life kept him from his family. He spoke on many occasions over multiple years about how he did not have enough time to see his wife and daughter as much as he wanted. He said he felt like his work life was "eating him up" and consuming far too much of his existence. In a telling exchange, he talked about the larger psychological impact of his heavy devotion to work, suggesting in a tentative way that maybe this situation is changeable. Anthony discussed a trip out of town he had taken the past weekend, how he had had a great time meeting new people, having fun, laughing. "It was so great to get away" from his job, from the pressures, from the "dullness and monotony." He said he realized how much he needs laughter and needs fun and how absent they are from his life. He wanted to bring that into his normal life instead of having to go away for that. Anthony said that he realizes how serious he is normally, at work and at home, and how serious he is even with the people he loves. As a defense lawyer he feels so much pressure to take care of problems, he explained, but he also takes that way of thinking home with him, feeling like he has to deal with his family in the same way. He concluded by saying that he thinks he doesn't have to do things like this all the time and doesn't want to go on like this.

This kind of statement, a typical one for Anthony and many other men in the movement, suggests the extent to which the men can feel that the kind of rationalized thinking that dominates their work life can come to infiltrate their personal lives as well. This is another indication of a Weberian critique of modern social dynamics, of the concept of the rationalization of thought that leads to the iron cage.[6]

Anthony is using the discourse of liberational masculinity (as explored in chapter 4) to criticize his experience of the work world and its impact on the rest of his life. He also opens the conceptual door to changing the dynamics in some way that addresses the causes of his negatively evaluated life situation. For about a year after this declaration, Anthony continued to complain about these issues. He experimented with a number of minor remedies that he hoped would change the situation but only had minor effect. He started to go to a massage therapist regularly to help with relaxation and stress reduction. He also tried getting up earlier in the morning to have time to start the day slowly, read the paper, and have more time with his family. Another effort was simply to try to mentally separate the work day from his time at home so he would not "bring home his work" and let it get in the way of his nonwork life.

Anthony reported some positive effects of these adjustments, but over the space of a year or two it appeared that he had not managed to solve the underlying problem. It became clear to him and other members that he was not attacking the cause of his dilemma, that is, the nature of his work life. After continued complaints and expressions of frustration at the ineffectiveness of his efforts, Anthony decided to cut back his work week. One night during a group meeting he explained his decision to work only four days a week. He explained that he "just can't take it anymore" and had decided he had to make a serious change. He said he had been looking over his finances and realized that he simply doesn't need to be making the kind of money he's currently making. He said he has savings and that it's unnecessary to be working this hard. The men were very excited for him and voiced their enthusiastic support. Dana even said later that "it's about time" Anthony did something like this.

As it turned out, even this change was not enough for Anthony. After further discussions in mythopoetic contexts over several months, Anthony announced that he was going to give up his law practice and work part-time as a consultant for someone else's firm. He indicated what a feeling of relief he felt to know that he's finally calling it quits. He said he is "filled with joy" whenever he thinks about it, that he can finally "get off the treadmill" and have time for his family and the rest of his life. The men were very supportive and seemed extremely pleased with Anthony's decision. One man called it "inspiring" and something that should make every member of the group think about his life and what changes he can make. Anthony thanked the group for all the support they'd given him and said, "I couldn't have done it without you."

Anthony's case is a very strong example of the kind of dramatic change brought about through involvement in the movement. Drawing in large part on the discourse of liberational masculinity constructed within the movement, he developed a specific critique of his life as being dominated by a dangerous work ethic and the need to achieve relentlessly in the public sphere. Through interaction in mythopoetic events over several years, he and other members were able to discuss and evaluate his dilemma and develop possible solutions. When those early, minor solutions did not address the problems to his satisfaction, the group beliefs and actions continued to encourage him to innovate new solutions. The end result is a dramatic change in his life that most probably will help fulfill his goals of being a better husband, a better father, and what he would consider a happier, healthier person in general. He has made the unusual decision to accept fewer material rewards and less professional prestige for the sake of alternative goals in his life. He appears to have succeeded, at least partially, in opting out of what the men identify as the modern rationalized drive for material success at the expense of family, love, emotional health, and other related ideals.

Sam provides another telling case study as one of the many men who has made dramatic life changes using mythopoetic movement beliefs. He was at one time an extremely rich and extremely busy businessman, but in midlife, under the guidance of movement ideals, he decided to completely change his life. Gradually, over a period of years in the mythopoetic men's movement, Sam became increasingly unsatisfied with the nature of his life. Like Anthony, he began to develop a critique of his life as overly focused on work and as psychologically and spiritually unhealthy. With the support of other men in the movement, he completely altered his life, opting for fewer material rewards and a more satisfying, less demanding professional life.

The case of Sam complements that of Anthony because Sam made the transformation prior to his inclusion in the population sample of this study. Anthony made the decision to change his life during the years of research of this study and it cannot be known for sure the long-term outcome of his new life course. Anthony's case thus provides a look at the process of decision making over several years inside the movement. But because Sam made his decision prior to the study, the data show the results of his change.

At the beginning of this study, Sam had been a member of the mythopoetic movement for three years. He had been involved in the movement in another state and upon moving recently he had joined the movement activities in the city of this study. At this point, Sam was beginning a new life. As he reported, he had completely abandoned his old life, inspired by the ideas of the movement. Sam explained that about a year ago he had decided to end his old life and start a new one. "I had it all," he said, listing his possessions: three houses in two states, seven cars, a motorcycle, two yachts, and more. He flew from place to place on a weekly basis, managing his construction business from one or another of several offices around the country. "I had more money than I could spend." The business was doing very well and his financial future looked bright. However, Sam slowly began to see the downside: he was never around for his wife and daughter.

Sam was constantly "stressed out" and "on the run." "If it was Tuesday, I was flying to Omaha. Thursday, Miami. Sometimes I'd stop in at home on the weekend to see my family," but then he would barely say "hi" and he was off to another site in another state. He realized over time that "this was no way to live." He talked about this realization a lot in the men's group he was in at that point and "they really helped me see how fucked up my life was." Sam started to "burn out," and one day realized he had to get rid of everything and leave his old life behind. Sam sold everything. He lost an incredible amount of money on the deal because he felt he had to get rid of everything immediately. He and his wife divorced, and his wife got half Sam's money and he gave a lot of it to his family and some friends. He then moved to a new city and started over. Sam credited his men's group with providing the inspiration and guidance that made it possible. He said he probably never would have "walked away" if it wasn't for them. Of all of the people he knew doing similar things with their lives then, he was the only one who had ever left the lifestyle behind completely, except for two friends who had retired.

In the new city Sam got a respectable job as a site manager for a local construction business, rented a medium-sized apartment in an upper-middle-class neighborhood, and created a new life. In an interview more than a year after the conversation in which he described leaving his old life, Sam discussed some of the changes he had made in his life.

> Well, it wasn't easy at first. I had a lot of nervous energy all the time. I felt like I was being lazy if I wasn't getting six things done at the same time. I still feel that way sometimes. And I can't afford the kind of things I used to buy all the time. But guess what? It was the best thing I ever did. It's like we talk about in group: "Be, Do, Have" instead of "Have, Do, Be." You know, it's all about priorities. I don't need all that shit I had. It just bought me headaches and an empty life. No wonder my marriage fell apart. I don't blame her for hating me. I was a shitty husband and a shitty father.

Sam struggled in mythopoetic contexts for years to change his way of thinking, as he discussed in our interview. This suggests how difficult it was for him to alter the internalized belief in a strong work ethic and transform the desire to be at the top of the financial hierarchy. The saying "Have, Do, Be" is a popular one in the movement, critiquing American thinking for emphasizing owning possessions as the first priority, doing activities as the second priority, and simply "being" as the last priority. Instead, the movement emphasizes the reverse priority list: "Be, Do, Have."

Later, almost a year after our interview, Sam discussed during a group meeting the problems he was having with making this transformation. Sam discussed his need to be constantly getting things done and said he has lists everywhere and is "addicted to Post-its." It's not that he necessarily doesn't like what he's doing, he explained, but that he wants to do things "at a sane pace." "I just need to slow down." He added that he is much better than he used to be about this sort of thing, but that he wants to go further. He talked about meditating more and not having such high standards for how much he should be getting done all the time. He said that he has trouble not doing things perfectly, even when it's not really necessary.

For Sam, this sentiment is a typical one, repeated a number of times in different ways throughout the period of this study. Like others discussed in this chapter, Sam had clearly internalized the values of industriousness, efficiency, and productivity. He struggled with his drive toward hard work and perfectionism. Still, he reported major progress with his efforts to change his participation in this cultural orientation. Much later, near the end of the study, he discussed how pleased he is with how his life is developing. He had met a woman and he was really looking forward to marrying Lisa in the fall, and they were enjoying the small house they had bought together. Sam said he's very happy with how much he's "slowed down" his life and that he feels like his lifestyle is "sane" for the first time in his life. He was happy with the new, deeper friendships he had developed in the past few years, and he thanked the group for being so supportive and helping him with all his "issues."

Sam's involvement with the mythopoetic men's movement was a major factor in his decision to reject the lifestyle he had led for most of his life. He then spent years in the local men's movement working in a more subtle way to purge himself of the work ethic values of constant productivity and efficiency. He reported what he frames as a healthier lifestyle more devoted to his new romantic relationship, close friendships, and the valuing of self-fulfillment and a reflective emotional life. Over the space of roughly seven years, Sam had dramatically reoriented his life according to central movement values.

Terrence provides a third representative case study of this kind of major life transformation motivated at least in part by cultural ideals developed in the mythopoetic men's movement. At the time of his inclusion in the present study, Terrence had been a member of the movement for about two years. He too decided to opt out of his lifestyle due in large part to his involvement in the movement. He had been a very successful businessman in creative development for television. In an interview, he told me his story.

Well, basically, I developed this idea for a new cable channel and was working on it for quite a while. Then the people backing it suddenly dropped the whole thing and I thought it was over. Lo and behold, a year later I get a call from someone who I had been working on the idea with and he says they went ahead and did it without us. I was fucking pissed off, as you can imagine. So, I found one of the best lawyers in the country that works on this sort of thing and sued the hell out of them. I got a block sum and a percentage of all the proceeds in the future. Well, that did it. I was out of there. I left the whole thing behind and started doing what I really wanted to do with my life. It's been great.

In a group meeting later that year, he spoke about what made him leave the business. He talked about how "horrible" the entertainment business is and described the people in control as "back-stabbing assholes" who will "do anything to make a buck." He was constantly complaining about it to his friends, his family, and the guys in his men's group. Terrence said that the group really pushed him to "take control of my life." They helped him realize, he said, that there was no way he was going to be able to change the basic nature of the business he was in and that he deserved better. He explained that it was making him "miserable" and he was turning into a "curmudgeonly old man," unable to enjoy life and "be a full person."

Like Anthony and Sam, Terrence cited the extent to which his work life way of thinking had begun to colonize his private life. Using central codes of the discourse of liberational masculinity, he constructed a critique of the culture of this business community and its effects upon him. With the help of his men's group, he developed a conception of himself as needing to leave this social realm and make a new life for himself.

Much later, when asked about how his life had been different in the past few years, Terrence said,

Basically, I've just been a much happier person. Like you've heard me say in group, I have a much simpler life and have slowed everything down. I can live on very little money, I have flexible hours and can do the kinds of things I've always wanted to. Like Watani, I can spend lots of time meditating, going to men's weekends and workshops, spending time with Sarah, and being creative in a lot of ways. It's such a sense of freedom compared to my old life ... Eventually I'm going to have to get a job again, because this money's not going to last forever, but I've made connections in various ways and I know I can find something in the New Age community or maybe my book will sell well, who knows. But I know I'll never go back to that hellish life I left behind.

Like Anthony and Sam, Terrence made a major life change in part due to his participation in the mythopoetic men's movement. He could have used the financial windfall he obtained to raise his level of spending or reinvested the money into a high-powered career to permanently raise his class position. Instead, he chose to use the windfall to drop out of the entertainment business in which he had been quite successful. Drawing in part from the discourse of liberational masculinity, Terrence negatively evaluated the traditional path of career success available to him. His moral construction of that option was so negative that he chose to throw away material and professional success in order to model his life on the ideals of the movement. In part using Watani as a model, he had created a new life that is centered around meditation, mythopoetic men's activities, time with his long-term girlfriend, writing, and other creative projects. For over five years after the change, he regularly reported very high levels of satisfaction with his new life.

In brief, three other distinct examples clearly display this model of dramatic life change inspired and guided to a significant degree by the values of the movement. These are the cases of Andrew, Kevin, and Dennis. Andrew's life path was strikingly similar to that of Sam and Terrence. Like many other men in the movement, Andrew also voluntarily opted out of a high-powered, successful career in order to scale back his life and pursue more intangible modes of fulfillment consistent with movement values. In his case, after years of involvement in the men's movement, Andrew left a profitable career in management and started a lower-level career in software design that left him with much more free time to pursue his interests in meditation, yoga, and poetry. His new career also gave him more time to develop a new romantic relationship and to spend more time with his ailing parents. As with the other members who changed their lives, he took a major pay cut to pursue these alternative life goals.

Kevin's case is similar except that the initial impetus for his change was not the movement and was not voluntary. He had a high-level career in real estate and was living a distinctly upper-class lifestyle when everything collapsed around him. His investments failed, he was unable to make payments on his houses, cars, and other debts, and he ultimately declared bankruptcy. Kevin and his wife divorced around this time. Kevin immediately started searching for a new direction in life, convinced that he needed to make fundamental changes. It was the mythopoetic movement that he credits with being a major force in allowing him to develop a new, much more satisfying life. In an interview he told me,

> I was totally lost at that point. I suddenly had no real idea where I was going. I just knew I wasn't going back. A friend of mine told me about these men's groups and that's when I joined. This group was such a godsend. The guys really helped me figure out what I wanted my life to be like. Looking back, I see what a sick lifestyle I had, always wheeling and dealing, more worried about money and work than my mental health and happiness.... And I was an asshole to people. I mean, if you don't love yourself, you can't love anyone else. I was a complete jerk to myself and to other people. I just thank God for the chance to start over.

Finally, Dennis shows another distinct variation on this model. He never had a particularly successful career but chose to use a financial windfall to change his life in a way that he interprets as a complete improvement. At the conclusion of this study, he had been a member of the movement off and on for about seven years. He made the change in his life during the time of the research and I was able to observe the process of him developing the idea to change his life within and with the input of his men's group and to see him actually bringing it about.

For years Dennis had been a delivery person for a major shipping firm. He described his work as a "dead-end job" that was "completely unsatisfying." It had no future, but it paid the bills. Dennis had been developing side projects centered around ecology and environmentalism. He had begun to lead children on nature hikes and river canoeing trips in which he would educate them about the ecology of the area and he had begun to do educational projects at a national park. Dennis was encouraged intermittently for more than two years by men in his group to quit his delivery job and try to make a full-time job out of some kind of independent career in the area of ecological education.

It was the death of Dennis's longtime partner to cancer that allowed him to pursue these suggestions. Dennis used the life insurance proceeds to buffer him during the interim period after he quit his delivery job and to help him start a new career in leading wildlife expeditions for children and adults and designing outdoor education programs for a national park. Also with group guidance, Dennis chose to lower his cost of living. At the conclusion of this study, he was about a year into his new life and extremely happy with the change. He credited his men's group with "getting him off his ass" and showing him that he did not have to go "the conventional route" in his life.[7]

## CREATING SMALLER MOVEMENT-INSPIRED CHANGES

Of course not all men in the movement make such life-altering changes in terms of the mythopoetic critique of an American work ethic. Many maintain their basic lifestyles but try to make smaller changes that they hope will bring about positive results vis-à-vis the values of the movement. Many men in the research sample fall into this category, including David, Nick, Henry, Doug, Tom, Victor, Gabriel, George, Alex, Talu, Carl, Richard, Dana, John, William, and Greg. For the sake of brevity, my analysis focuses on three cases that offer a representative spectrum of techniques within this approach. Examining the actions of David, Nick, and Henry allows an understanding of typical uses of these ideas to create smaller yet significant life changes.

David was part of the sample population for the entire eight years of my research. He is a modestly successful film director, screenwriter, and actor; one film that he wrote and directed had midlevel release throughout the United States and Europe. Throughout the time of the study, David grappled with the dilemma of how to live what he considered to be a healthy, happy life in line with mythopoetic values while being involved in the film industry, which he portrayed quite critically.

Early in my study David talked during a group discussion about the film industry and its effects on his life. He spoke about his frustration with making films because all the guys he has to deal with are "professional liars." He called them "money-grubbing, cheap, greedy con artists" who are basically "Mafia swindlers." He said they'll "use you," "tell you anything," and then "back-stab you." "I don't want this energy in my life. I don't need it." But David said he gets "sucked into their game." He said they smile, shake your hand and you know "it's all lies." It's a whole "capitalist system," he declared, in which everyone wants to scramble their way to the top, get all the money and power, and kick everyone else down. He explained that his friend was telling him how there's two structures to an organization: pyramid and spider web, in which the pyramid is the "capitalist vicious competition game" and the spider web is the more "cooperative" system where everyone works together, is interrelated, and needs each other. The spider web system is what he wants. He said he's planning on finishing this film he's working on now and then after that only making "little independent films" so he doesn't have to "deal with these people."

Immediately after David's monologue, Watani began a physical exercise designed to help David "get in touch with" his emotions so that he can understand them better and address them proactively to get at the underlying problems. Watani placed the members of the group around David told them to squeeze into him so that he had trouble moving. Watani said that we are all the sleazy guys in the industry, that we are holding you back, lying to you, restricting you, keeping you from living truly. People jumped in: "You're nothing, man. You have to do what we say." "You have to believe us because you don't know any better." Watani instructed us to push David and told David to fight back. It got very physical, but eventually David was able to break away from the group's physical hold on him. He was very angry. We all surrounded him and did the same thing again. David broke out again but then slumped over into full-throated sobbing, tears running down his face. He said through his tears, "I can't take it... It's not fair... I can't stand it any more." After David settled down, the men supported him, gave him hugs, and congratulated him for working well through the exercise.

This kind of physical exercise meant to stimulate emotions is a regular, though relatively infrequent, practice during group meetings. Though the exact format varies, it is generally successful at evoking strong feelings about the subject at hand. In this case David thanked the group afterward and said that the exercise really "got me in touch with what was going on about this." He then said that he had to do something about this because he "can't take it much longer."

Over time, David developed his critique of the film industry and of American society. He intermittently reported various efforts with trying to be honest and sincere in the industry. It was clearly a struggle for him to try to succeed within that realm while still trying to uphold mythopoetic values. About a year after the above events, he discussed his understanding of modern culture and his work. At that point in the meeting, the group was talking about commitment, responsibility, and honesty. David said it's all about "growing up" and "maturity." He declared that "we have an adolescent culture" in which "no one takes responsibility." He cited today's male movie stars, saying they are just boys who are immature. Later in the same night David explained how he gets drawn into the industry's way of thinking, explaining that he's good at "scheming," "networking," calling people up, making connections. He said he has to do it, "but I hate it" because it's "so surface, so dishonest." He explained that he has to do it for his work but that he is trying to do it less, to avoid people who are like this, to work with better people, and to diplomatically "call people on their bullshit."

Taking mythopoetic values into the public, workplace realm is clearly a challenge for David, as it is in various ways for other men as well. The men regularly show that the workplace ways of thinking and cultural values clash with the discourse of liberation masculinity and other critical ideology from the movement. Almost a year after the meeting just discussed, David discussed this issue again and how helpful the group had been. He also got some advice from Watani and others that he later followed. David told a story of how industry people swindled him out of $1.5 million that had been promised for his movie. He said they're "all liars," "power hungry," and "always trying to make money." He criticized how "capitalist" the business is and how powerless they make him feel when they push him around, taking control out of his hands. For example, he explained, they regularly call him and say they need a decision made in half an hour when it isn't even his place to make the decision and they know what he's going to say regardless. He said they're just "covering their asses." David got increasingly angry, and later said how helpful it had been to be discussing these issues regularly with the group so that he can figure out how to deal with them. He said it would be helpful the next morning when he had an "eleven-way conference call over three continents." Watani and others told David that he needed a mentor, someone who's been through all this before and can give him tips. They told him, "You're a novice," "you're naïve," "you need guidance from an elder."

In keeping with his own earlier comment on the importance of taking responsibility, David did not blame only others for this professional dynamic. Seven months later, David discussed a way in which his own perspective might be getting in the way of his progress with these dilemmas. He admits that he always wants more and needs to learn when to stop and be satisfied with what he has. This follows the group tenet encouraging members to examine how they themselves contribute to a situation and what they can do to help solve the problem.

David explicated his understanding of this idea in an interview almost a year later. "I guess I've been realizing over time that I'm part of the problem. I can't be a control freak and expect everything to be done my way. I'm sort of a perfectionist sometimes, but I have to let other people have their say, even if they're wrong. [*laughs*] Films are collaborative efforts and I have to roll with the flow sometimes. But that doesn't mean they're not assholes!" Later in the same interview, when asked if the group had had any other impact on his professional dilemmas, David said,

> Well of course. I mean, you've been there for the whole thing. It's been great to get perspective on things in group. The guys have shown me ways I can be more honest and straightforward and still get my films made. I take a lot less shit than I used to, and I feel more mature about the whole thing. You know, they respect you if you don't just let them screw you over all the time. And I've learned who to avoid and who I can trust. I do my bit to make things a little better, but there's no way to change some of those guys.

David has clearly made some practical progress with these central difficulties in his work life. While he has not dramatically altered his life, he reports significant steps forward. During the eight years in which he was part of the study, he has clearly used mythopoetic ideals to help him construct a critique of key dynamics of his professional life. Then, going beyond this, he reports actually improving these issues to some degree with the direct help of his men's group. It appears that David has learned to work more cooperatively and to not hold himself and his work to quite such "pathologically high standards." In this way, he has unlearned key elements of what the men identify as a destructive work ethic. Further, in conjunction with his men's group and central movement values, he seems to have been able to develop methods with which to create more honest, straightforward, and trusting interactions in his professional career.

Nick is a second telling case of a man in the movement who struggled in group meetings with work issues and had successfully made significant changes along the lines of mythopoetic values. Nick identified himself as a "workaholic" who had internalized a dominant American work ethic that he identifies as destructive to him and those in his life.

By the end of this study, Nick had been a member of the mythopoetic men's movement for almost eight years. During the four years in which he was part of the study population, he regularly discussed his work life dilemmas and worked to make changes. He addressed two major issues: the quantity of time spent on work and the emotional dynamics of his work experience.

Nick regularly complained about the high percentage of his life devoted to work. He repeatedly said that it was "taking over" his life and leaving very little time and energy for his relationship with his wife and for other parts of his personal life. On a weekend mythopoetic campout, I taped the following lengthy interaction, which shows Nick and others constructing a way of understanding the situation and ways to change it.

> MARIO: As time goes by, that will gel. As long as I'm searching for it and I keep my mind open, it will happen.
>
> DENNIS: The passion you're looking for may be something you're doing. Do you love the work you're doing?
>
> MARIO: Yeah, but . . .
>
> DENNIS: That doesn't make you a whole person.
>
> MARIO: Right.
>
> DENNIS: But you spend eight, ten, twelve hours a day doing it. And you love doing that. But you need more.
>
> MARIO: I don't want my work to consume me.
>
> NICK: Look at all the distractions there are out there. Like look at all those special interest magazines. Like mountain climbing, rock climbing, diving, you know, snorkeling, windsurfing. Everything's turned into an industry. But that's fine. Because they're super passions for many people so they develop magazines and networks of people for it, but they're all open to people like you and I, and they really get into it. I know a guy who does it for windsurfing. He goes out twice a month and just windsurfs all day. He's completely flipped out about it. I have absolutely no interest in doing it, but three years ago, I could never see myself touching a golf club, and now I go to the range and slip off whenever I can to play. So who knows. You gotta really open your mind."
>
> MARIO: That's right. I've really got to do that.
>
> DENNIS: You've really got to be open to yourself. That's something I'm always trying to do. I realize now that there's a lot of different sides to me. And I always try to bring that into my life. I question whether I'm doing enough, you know?
>
> NICK: It all depends. For me, I do it for escapism. It's so powerful for me, the mysticism of hitting it into that hole. Getting from this point to this point and getting it into that hole and all that it's going to entail. I don't think about shit when I'm doing that. And that's so powerful.
>
> DENNIS: That's the main thing. You've got to find something, whatever it is, golfing or anything else. You've got to find a thing where you don't think of anything else. I mean, meditation, that's what it is.

NICK: Mario, how much of that do you have? None.

...

WATANI: Look at your social consciousness. Look at society, the environment, your spirituality, your personal growth. Don't just limit yourself to recreation and activities. It can all be the same thing ... take the Mentor Project downtown. It's with these kids who are really in need of capable mentoring. And it doesn't mean you can't bring sports into it in the form of a game or whatever.

In this interaction, the men are constructing a notion of the importance of passion in one's personal life. While they do not directly advocate changes in the professional realm here, they are clearly suggesting a change in the relative priority of work life versus personal life. Certainly playing golf is not a radical alteration of one's life, but one gets the sense from Nick's poetic description that it really does make a difference in his experience of life. It is clear that the men are addressing their self-professed "workaholic" tendencies in at least somewhat productive ways. The men are sharing the lessons they feel they have learned and encouraging other men to make perhaps relatively minor yet potentially effective alterations in the way they live their lives.

About a year later, Nick did in fact pursue the idea of mentoring. During a group meeting, he explained what a difference it has made in his life and in the life of his nephew, whose parents' divorce had been very hard on him, especially given that his mother and father had apparently been less-than-model parents. Nick explained how much it meant for him to be able to spend so much time with his nephew. It has been "extremely fulfilling," he said, to be able to "give back to the younger generation" and teach his nephew some of the lessons that he'd learned and that he wishes someone had taught him when he was a kid. Nick said it's a "great excuse" to skip out of work early and do something that's "emotionally fulfilling."

Nick later even took his nephew on a mythopoetic men's campout and reported that it was "a great experience" and that his nephew thought it was "awesome." Clearly his group has had an effect on Nick, encouraging and supporting him in his actions to raise the priority of his personal life while simultaneously lowering the priority of his professional life. The change he has made is not a radical one, but it is a significant one nonetheless.

Nick's focus on work and the way he runs his construction business was a topic of discussion on a number of occasions over the years. In a typical exchange, the men in his group encouraged him to change his behavior, suggesting that he relax about his business and "let it run itself" a little bit, instead of constantly "micromanaging" everything. They told him he should spend more time with his family, golf more, and work fewer hours.

A year later, group members developed this point further, arguing forcefully that Nick should alter the way he manages his business. They called him "overly controlling" and "obsessive" about running everything himself, and they criticized him for not trusting others and not letting go of direct control over anything. Apparently Nick's company does millions of dollars of business a year, and the group members question why he tries to handle such a big operation almost by himself. Nick got defensive and said he knows it's a problem and that he's getting a new secretary, which he hoped would lighten the load. People pushed him to hire a real assistant, a controller to help run the company, saying that he's "stupid not to" and that he can afford one despite the fact that he thinks he can't. Mario was also confronted with the same issues by Anthony and others, because he owns a large chunk of a successful upscale hotel and yet has no secretary.

In fact, that year Nick did hire a controller and then reported significant improvements in his workload and the corresponding emotional dynamics of his work life. It is important to note that this is essentially another instance of a man taking a cut in pay in order to pursue what he sees as a healthier life that involves more time with his family and more personal time. As the sole owner of the business, the salary of a new employee comes out of Nick's pocket via his company. The goal of hiring a controller was not to make the business more profitable but, rather, to reduce Nick's workload. Nick has, in effect, created a job for someone else so that he is no longer doing two jobs at once. Nick conceptualizes the move as a direct tradeoff of money for emotional health, changing what had been identified in many different ways as the culturally ingrained tradeoff of emotional health for money.

Nick also struggled with some changes regarding the nature of professional relationships forged in the workplace. He identified difficulties with integrity, other business ethics, and the fear of failure. In a group meeting, he explained that he's "a nice guy" on the job. He promises too much to people and then can't always deliver. Anthony, Mario, and I pointed out that he is guilty of this in personal interactions as well, and two or three members criticized him for not returning phone calls in a timely way. Nick talked about procrastination in business dealings and about feeling constantly overwhelmed. He said he feels like "a guy spinning plates" who has to "run around frenetically" keeping all the plates spinning and that he feels like "disaster is always looming." As a contractor, he said, he has to promise everything to everyone. He admitted that he feels like he has to lie sometimes to get a contract, in order to try to stay competitive with all the other guys who are lying even more. He said he's ashamed about it but can't figure out what to do.

Nick has a distinct cultural value dilemma. He is committed to mythopoetic beliefs but also feels that he has to make questionable promises and even outright lie to stay competitive. He is in a situation of cultural contradiction with which he is clearly not happy. But the topic at the group meeting changed, Nick's problem was shelved, and Nick continued in the same liminal, problematic state.

A month later, however, Nick brought up the topic again in a group meeting. This time the group got more deeply involved in trying to suggest changes in Nick's life that they hope will solve the dilemma in a way consistent with movement values. Nick reported that he had made "a good breakthrough" last night with his therapist and his wife related to the work issues he'd been talking about in group. It's summed up, he explained, in the saying, "If someone can't say 'No,' then their 'Yes'es become meaningless." He said that he's realizing that he needs to learn how to be honest about whether he can really do something for someone and that he has to stop saying "yes" just to please people and keep them "connected to me." He explains that in building, it's a competition and you don't want to say "no" and send customers to a competitor because then you've lost them altogether. He says you'd rather say "yes" and even make promises you know you can't fulfill because then you know you've got them and you can deal with the details later. The problem, he explained, is that it starts to backfire and you lose customers because you can't deliver. He added that you let down friends and family when you do it in your personal life.

Watani told Nick that he thinks he wants people to like him, that Nick wants them to think highly of him and if he makes promises, then he's "got them hooked." Nick agreed. Dana told Nick that it seems like there's a real sense of lack of completeness, lack of wholeness, and lack of confidence in his own goodness, like Nick needs to convince others to like him. Kevin agreed, saying that Nick has to perform to please them and there's a sense that he thinks he's not good enough. Watani told Nick that he knows Nick is aware of this issue and that the group has talked about it before, but that Nick has to be "ready to risk the relationship," to take the chance of not saying "yes," of not taking the easy way out and pleasing everyone. Kevin said, "You're good enough, Nick," that he knows the group members all think that, and that Kevin likes Nick as he is. Kevin hugs Nick.

While this kind of heavy-handed "New Age," pop psychology may not be appealing to everybody, it seems to have its intended effect in the mythopoetic context. Nick has a significant dilemma here, torn as he is between what he sees as the demands of market competition and his commitment to mythopoetic values. He lives his professional life directly in the public sphere of the market economy, which is devoted in a fundamental way to competition and profitability. Values of integrity, emotional openness, and mutual support often take second priority.

However, combating the apparent market pressures does not fall solely to his own moral consciousness as developed in part in the men's movement. In fact, his men's group very actively criticizes his behavior, challenging him to rise to the values of the movement. In line with these beliefs, he also reports the earnest involvement of his individual therapist and his wife, who act as a complement to the movement here. Clearly there is a dynamic feedback cycle occurring in which he raises issues in the group, in therapy, and with his wife in a fluid and mutually reinforcing way.

Also shown here is the way that patterns of thinking developed in the workplace are seen as colonizing one's personal life. Nick conceptualizes this competitive, disingenuous way of thinking and acting as being the creation of the market environment, which then in turn infiltrates his personal life. He speaks of letting down friends and family through the same process of making promises on which he cannot deliver. Members of the group then construct an understanding of this dynamic as negative, given the central cultural beliefs of the group, regardless of the context in which it occurs. In typical logic, they interpret it in an individualistic, psychological way as a fundamental flaw in Nick's consciousness. They clearly challenge him to rise about this weakness, suggesting that it is unnecessary and destructive to his own emotional health and personal well-being.

This topic came up again a number of times during the following three years of the study. The issues were framed similarly, and Nick intermittently reported attempts to change the dynamic. He said that he is trying to be more careful not to mislead customers in general and not to lie. He reported that he is trying to explain to customers that jobs take time and money and that they should not be "taken in" by other contractors who may be willing to lie and underestimate costs and completion time estimates. He explained that he has probably lost some customers this way but feels much better about the business and himself when he is honest. He also reported some success in reducing this kind of behavior in his personal life.

Nick has clearly made some changes in the style of his business dealings according to mythopoetic values. He understands these social dynamics in a different way because of the movement, and he has changed his life to some extent as a result. This adds to the other changes he has made in terms of working fewer hours, sharing job responsibilities, and generally reducing the priority of his professional life relative to his personal life. According to his reports, others have also benefited from these changes, including his wife, his nephew, the rest of his family, his coworkers, and, presumably, his clients.[8]

The third and last case study of significant, yet not dramatically life-altering, change is that of Henry. Over the years of the study, Henry made what he regards as distinctly positive changes regarding work and his professional life. He did so in close consultation with his men's group, which has repeatedly offered him typically mythopoetic visions of new directions in his life. Guided by movement ideals, he and his group succeeded in institutionalizing distinct revisions in the way he structures his public and private life.

Henry was a member of the research population for the last five years of the study. When he joined his men's group, Henry worked as a receptionist for an auto towing company and struggling as a part-time screenwriter, actor, and director. He was twenty-nine years old and repeatedly expressed dissatisfaction with his work life. He felt that his life lacked direction, and he was unsure about his future. In a meeting about a year into his involvement in the mythopoetic movement, Henry explained that he wants attention and respect. He wants to "put down his burden." He said that he always takes on unnecessary responsibility, leading to disappointment. He told a story from childhood of a huge mess that his brother made with corn flakes and Kool-Aid and how he took the blame for his brother. He explained that he has done things like that his entire life, taking on burdens for other people that end up hurting him and in many cases not really helping the other person. He said he is a "performer," always acting to try to get attention and positive feedback.

Watani told Henry that attention can be an addiction, just like heroin. Henry said that he's tired of "not being heard" and being underappreciated. He wants to "find his path," to "just do it" and take charge and initiative in his life. He wants not to specifically look for approval but to just naturally get it for doing a good job at things. Henry said that even in group he always looks for approval. The men supported Henry and encouraged him to go out and make his life work according to his values and sincere goals.

Two weeks later, Henry brought this issue up in the group again, saying that he feels like he hangs back, letting his "old baggage" slow him down in all the parts of his life. He wants to "take charge," "be heard," and "stand up" for himself. He wants "power," "respect," and "to be taken seriously." Watani then took Henry through an exercise designed to create change through group dynamics. Watani told Henry to go around the room and tell each member what he needs in order to encourage his growth. To me he said, "I need you to ... [*pause*] This is really scary." Watani encouraged Henry to continue. "I need you to keep me involved," to "hit me" and tell me to "say what I'm thinking." He told Paul to "kick my ass," and he told Scott to "needle me," "criticize me," "keep me honest," and "go after me." Scott said that he also wants to "honor" him, to "love" him, and that he needs to be able to show "his soft side" and his weakness. Paul agreed that it's important to show your full self. Henry continued around the room asking people to not "coddle" him and not always take his side. At the end, Henry said that he needs to "come out" and "demand to be heard," be assertive and take charge.

After the group meeting ended that night, Henry and I talked outside. He discussed these issues specifically with respect to his screenwriting group. Henry talked about feelings of inferiority and feeling like "I don't deserve this." He said that having the group talking stick at home shows him that "the men trust me with this" and that he really is a central part of the group and a full member. He explained that just recently he had been taking charge in his screenwriting group. He said he's done with them thinking of themselves as "just some college kids." "I come all this way," he explained, and present "all these ideas" and they "just shoot them down" and then "we bullshit for hours." "My life isn't about that any more. I need to get things done." He explained that he put his foot down and told them what he thought and what he needed. "I kicked their ass." They were surprised and shocked, he reported, but they listened and "finally I got my point across."

Henry is already making changes in his professional life consistent with movement values that he has picked up in the first year of his participation. At various points over the first few years of his membership, other men in his group congratulated him for steps he is taking in "growing up," becoming more "mature," and "taking charge" of his life. Henry was repeatedly encouraged to become proactive about developing his "life path," both public and private, both professional and personal. They urged him to make his work life "meaningful" and "an expression of his true self."

After about two years in the movement, Henry discussed his feelings about professional success and productivity during a group meeting. Henry complained about how much time he has to spend just making money to survive and how much he hates his receptionist job. He said he feels "so lazy" and "unproductive." "I feel like shit," he exclaimed, because he can't get any screenwriting done. He explained that he feels "inadequate" and "ashamed." Kevin questioned him, pointing out that he had had some success recently with one of his screenplays getting serious attention from some small production companies. Henry unenthusiastically agreed, and Kevin suggested that Henry may be "afraid of success" and asks him whether he feels like he "doesn't deserve it." Henry quietly agreed that that might be happening. Kevin asked him why he might feel that way and suggested that he finish the sentence "I don't deserve success because ...." Henry responded, "I don't deserve success because ... I'm lazy ... because ... I'm not focused...." Watani encouraged him to "go deeper." Henry said, "because ... I'm short ... because I'm not good enough." After a long pause, he explained that he thinks that he doesn't feel fully grown up yet, that he doesn't have the confidence and strength. He was having trouble saying all of this, and then he said softly, "I guess I just don't feel like a man." Kevin talked about how the group didn't see him in these negative terms and about how Henry's "putting labels" on himself. Members expressed agreement. Watani weighed in, declaring that Henry needs to free himself of these labels and "quiet those voices in your head," that he needs to stop "judging" himself and go out and make his life the way he wants it. "Follow your path," Watani said, arguing that Henry needs to find work that really fulfills him and does more than just pay the bills.

This topic came up again with Henry several times in the following year or so, and he announced one night that he really needs to quit his towing company job. He explained that his screenwriting is going well, though it is still not a source of income and that he is looking into teaching, which is something he has always wanted to do some day. Three weeks later, he reported the latest results. Henry very excitedly told the group that he finally quit his towing company job. He explained "what a relief" it was to "get out of there" and how enthusiastic he is about his new job teaching part-time in the public grade school system. He talked about how much he's "always loved kids" and how much more fulfilling the work is. He said he's been "facing his fears" about being "an authority figure" and what a thrill it is to be a part of the kids' lives. He thanked the guys in the group for helping him develop the "confidence" and "strength" to leave his old job and try something completely new. He said, "I couldn't have done it without you guys" and that it's in group that he fully realized that he should and could "follow my heart" and look for work that was emotionally satisfying and where he could feel like he was giving something to the world. He said it's been "scary" but that it looks like it's going to work out well.

Over the next two years, Henry talked repeatedly about his teaching experiences and reported his satisfaction with the work, especially as he gained experience, skills, and confidence. He said that his screenwriting was going better because the teaching "keeps me open," "gives me ideas," and "gets my creative juices flowing" as opposed to his old towing company job, which "shut me down" and "left me dead at the end of the day."

At the end of the study, Henry had still not had any of his screenplays selected for a major production. However, he had made a short film that won two small awards, he reported making new connections within the industry, and he felt that his writing was improving. Regardless of the exact level of his success with his screenwriting efforts, Henry had clearly changed his professional life for the better through his participation with the movement. He reports more confidence and proactive assertiveness in his work-related dealings, and he has changed his standards for work satisfaction, helping him quit an unfulfilling job and start a new part-time career track with which he is very happy. He reports higher levels of creativity and other improvements in his unpaid screenwriting career. Henry directly credits his men's group with helping him develop these positive changes. It is clear that mythopoetic beliefs have been a driving force in helping him create a work life that prioritizes those ideals over others.

## CONCLUSION

The men of the mythopoetic men's movement have constructed a critique of what they see as a destructive work ethic that is prevalent in American culture. Together in group meetings, retreats, workshops, and informal gatherings, they have developed an understanding of modernity that directly opposes many central cultural tenets of American society. They question what they see as the dominant ethos of material success, the life-track formula of continual hard work leading to increasing levels of professional achievement and material prosperity.

However, this is not merely an impersonal political critique; they tend to see themselves as the carriers of this institutionalized ethos. That is, in the same way that they see the dominant discourse of masculinity, they see the work ethic as hegemonic and themselves as its previously unwitting agents. They construct an understanding of themselves as having internalized this set of cultural beliefs and enacted it for most of their lives. They see their involvement in the movement as directly motivated by the desire to purge themselves of this element of their identities. They want to resocialize themselves in a sense, to free themselves of what they identify as a destructive code of existence. It is an individualistic and social-psychological critique. They point to the negative effects in their own lives of this dominant ethos. They question whether material success is worth the price that must be paid and whether the endless striving to reach the top of the hierarchy is prohibitively destructive of emotional health. They criticize the power of workplace ways of thinking to colonize the private realm and damage personal relationships, and they question the fundamental meaning of success and redefine it away from material ideals toward more emotional ideals, including family, creativity, and spirituality.

This is a neo-Weberian critique that, while far from fully theorized, nonetheless criticizes what can be seen as the spirit of capitalism and rationalization. This is combined with a "New Age" sensibility that prioritizes emotional fulfillment, love, and alternative spirituality. It is clearly not a Marxist critique, as the questioning of such dynamics as class inequality, property relations, and exploitation is absent. Rather, it calls into question beliefs central to Western culture and is a significant cultural critique with a social-psychological basis.

These socially constructed cultural ideals of the men's groups are then acted upon in concrete ways. The movement is dedicated to being more than simply a context for discussion. Mythopoetic groups emphasize the importance of members creating changes in their lives stemming directly from understandings constructed within movement contexts. Each member is encouraged to find his own specific applications of movement ideals and to institutionalize them in his life.

For some members of the groups this means dramatic, life-altering changes. As I explored earlier in this chapter, a number of men in Watani's groups significantly transform their lives, abandoning highly successful careers in midstride in order to pursue alternative visions of social existence. For most of these men, this meant a significant step down in the social hierarchy in terms of money, property, financial security, and professional prestige. Despite this, they report high levels of satisfaction with their new developments, crediting the movement with helping them to both conceptualize the changes and institutionalize them.

Of course the majority of movement participants developed less dramatic changes in their lives. Many of the men realized changes that, while not completely transforming their lives, created significant results. Members scaled back work schedules, sacrificing material rewards in favor of emotional rewards; they made alterations in the nature of their workplace experience; they shifted career tracks to emphasize movement ideals; and they changed the ways they interacted with coworkers and clients.

Of course a small percentage of men in the groups I observed fell into neither of these categories, either leaving the movement for various reasons or being new members who had yet to institutionalize any significant changes with respect to these issues of work and professional achievement. Nonetheless, those who did not report any changes in these terms made up a very small proportion of the study population and were clearly the exception to the rule. Thus, it is safe to conclude that the mythopoetic men's movement is fulfilling its own goals of developing a critique of the American work ethic and what is seen as the culture of capitalism. The movement then follows up this critique by encouraging and guiding men in institutionalizing corresponding concrete changes in their lives.

The mythopoetic men's movement is an unusual social movement in that it does not pursue structural changes in the economic, political, or legal spheres. It is a strange phenomenon: a gender movement that works neither for nor against greater gender equality. It is certainly not a feminist movement, though it does have some feminist qualities. It is not accurately described as a backlash *against* feminism either, though it is content to largely ignore issues of women's equality. It is not a conservative movement overall, but neither is it a particularly progressive one. Rather, the mythopoetic men's movement focuses on creating social change one man at a time in a psychological and cultural way that has no macrolevel agenda for social change. The movement seeks to undermine self-identified dominant cultural discourses for the sake of ideals of love, family, relationships, creativity, and spirituality. These changes, as they are institutionalized in men's lives, then in turn affect others, in a ripple-effect pattern that appears to have had significant results for countless wives, girlfriends, children, parents, friends, coworkers, and clients. While it is impossible to measure the exact macroeffects of the movement, it is clear that the more than one hundred thousand men in the movement have changed the lives of many people in addition to themselves. It is reasonable to conclude that, along with the significant media coverage of the movement, these men have made subtle, yet notable changes in the cultural landscape of contemporary America. They have planted seeds that may continue to contribute to the ongoing changes in society with respect to gender, emotional dynamics, and alternative definitions of success. The movement is thus an example of how structured cultural ideals, constructed in face-to-face interaction, can, under certain circumstances, significantly change social arrangements, both in the public and private spheres.

## NOTES

1. Note that this critique is focused predominantly on their own self-interests. Primarily, the vision identifies the negative outcomes, *for themselves,* of professional and economic success. In this way, it is a very different political understanding than that focusing on distributive injustice and unequal access to scarce resources. On one level, this can be criticized as a very self-centered conservative analysis; on another level, it is a systematic radical critique, suggesting that the cultural system of capitalism is not even desirable for those in the upper tiers of the economy.

2. It is interesting to note that their critique is thus not a political one, in the traditional sense of the term. It is not connected in any real way to the institutional political sphere and there is no conceptualization of public ways to address the problem. Given the emotional focus of their perspective, they are left with only individualistic solutions.

3. From time to time the men make explicit references to a critical understanding of hegemonic masculinity and the dominant culture as being two sides of the same coin. This is made clear in chapter 4 in terms of the connections made between the dominant values of public institutions and the codes of hegemonic masculinity. Here the idea is developed that to be a good worker is to be a good man, and vice versa.

4. It should be noted that the men have vague ideas of a different macrosocial order developing in the future. They see society as fundamentally flawed, and they hope for dramatic change in the distant future. However, they have no specific plan for how to bring this about. They do not connect their critique to any political processes that might address the problem on a public level.

5. Watani is an "equal opportunity" cultural innovator. While he draws much of his material from Native American and Eastern spiritual traditions, he also integrates insights from the popular media, including recent movies, television shows, songs, advertising, and the news media. This accords with his role as organic intellectual, as discussed in chapter 3; he interprets the ideas of movement high intellectuals and makes them accessible to the rank-and-file members of the movement in a way that speaks to their immediate life experiences.

6. One is also reminded of Jürgen Habermas's (1984, 1987) argument concerning the colonization of the lifeworld by system logic.

7. These case studies are intentionally depicted in a succinct manner in order to avoid repetition and to develop a more concise, focused analysis. In every case, there is much more data supporting the argument from both group context observations and interviews.

8. In unstructured interactions, this has been supported through informal discussions with Nick's wife at two different social events that were not formal mythopoetic events. I also had the chance to talk privately with one of the men who works for him, who confirmed some of the positive changes that Nick had discussed during group meetings and interviews.

# 6

# Conclusion

This study contributes to several different fields in a number of focused ways. On an empirical level, the study promotes a deeper understanding of the mythopoetic men's movement. On a theoretical level, the project primarily addresses the field of cultural sociology, building on the most recent work in order to add to this growing area of scholarship. The use of the cultural discourse perspective begun by Alexander (1992) is expanded and generalized through the analysis of the evaluative framework of mythopoetic masculinity. Considerations of power, hegemony, social control, and social change have been integrated into the approach without undermining the fundamental commitment to a cultural perspective and correspondingly without falling into the trap of materialist analysis. Moreover, this project makes a step in the direction of more fully integrating issues of contingency and agency into cultural work through the use of ethnography to study small-scale face-to-face interaction. The project contributes in a small way to ongoing attempts toward synthesis of the micro/macro divide and the structure/agency dichotomy.

This project also contributes to the study of masculinity and of gender more generally. Understanding the mythopoetic men's movement suggests new ways to think about masculinity and gender, including how gender identity is internally structured and the product of situated interaction mediated through socially constructed culture structures. This suggests ways in which gender is an ongoing achievement that is guided by macrolevel cultural/historical processes while it is simultaneously negotiated on the face-to-face interactive level.

The study also attempts to contribute to the field of microsociology, specifically ethnographic analysis and small group interaction.

My analysis shows that it is possible to develop fully cultural work using interactional data gleaned from ethnographic methods. This helps opens up the study of face-to-face interaction to a broader range of analysis, freeing it from the strictly micro focus that has been the traditional approach. I also show that it is possible to do this in a nonfunctionalist way that preserves the appreciation of contingency and individual agency that has traditionally been the strength of microlevel work and a weakness of functionalism. Relatedly, my research tries to show how issues of power can be analyzed without losing the individual-level sensitivity that is so often missing in Marxist and other macrolevel power-oriented work. In general, macroanalyses are limited in their analytical power in that they cannot understand in a subtle way the issues of individual motivation that, in the aggregate, ultimately constitute any larger organization, movement, or social structure and significantly affect its future. Using a fully interactive as well as cultural perspective allows the understanding of the role of meaning in providing the moral drive that is a significant determinant of the character and future of any larger social entity.

## THE MYTHOPOETIC MEN'S MOVEMENT

On the empirical level, this study aims to fill gaps left by previous research on the mythopoetic men's movement. Previous work has generally left unexamined the construction of meaning in real-life interaction within movement contexts and has often failed to look at how the movement is correspondingly changing the lives of the participants. The primary reason for this is methodological. Scholars have almost always chosen a content analysis approach, limiting their research to the published writings of movement high intellectuals. While this has certainly been a worthwhile inquiry, it leaves unexplored what is actually happening within the movement. This requires direct, in-person research such as interviews or participant observation. Looked at on this level of complexity, a much fuller story emerges. For instance, the data in chapter 3 make it clear that the group leader is a kind of organic intellectual, creatively and forcefully shaping movement ideas. Leaders use their local power to push, pressure, and even manipulate members to think and act according to their visions. Chapter 4 offers another example of this, as the data show that the participants are creatively constructing a new cultural discourse that contains key counterhegemonic elements. This is something they have produced in interaction (mostly in small group settings), not absorbed from texts. And in chapter 5 we see this again in another way as the men create critical ideas about work and economics and then change their lives accordingly. Ethnographic research, not just analysis of movement texts, was necessary to discover these dynamics at this level of detail and complexity.

A second major reason that previous work has overlooked many of these issues is that previous work has limited itself to constructing a political criticism of the movement. There are certainly a number of conservative and antifeminist ideas in the movement, including the celebration of certain characteristics of traditional masculinity as well as some essentialist ideas about gender. These are clearly contained in the guiding texts of the movement and played out in various ways within the movement. However, stopping at this critique tells only part of the story. As I show in chapters 3, 4, and 5, there is much more happening within the movement, including some ideas of a moderately liberal or progressive character and some overlaps with ideas from the feminist movement. The men clearly criticize hegemonic masculinity and are looking for new ways to be men in contemporary society. They question the traditional male preoccupation with prestige and economic success and change their lives accordingly. On the other hand, this movement certainly ignores a wide range of central feminist ideals. It pays little attention to inequalities and discrimination, including those based on gender, race, class, and sexual orientation. It does not actively seek to change the legal, political, or economic systems on the macro level. Instead, it seeks change on the micro level, creating new cultural and psychological conceptualizations that change one man at a time. This then affects others like ripples on a pond, spreading well beyond the immediate context of the movement. It can be seen as a significant "seed" movement, introducing new ideas into the larger culture.

The mythopoetic men's movement challenges what it sees as the dominant discourse of gender in general and masculinity in particular. As such, it is part of the unfolding history of social change with respect to gender. It is a part of the growing community of men who are questioning and changing masculinity in new ways. Men in the movement are engaged in a previously almost unthinkable undertaking—they are disassembling their own dominant identity patterns that have, in one way or another, been part of the patriarchal makeup of almost all known cultures throughout history.

Specifically, the men have helped construct a complex culture structure, the discourse of mythopoetic masculinity, that simultaneously attacks what they see as hegemonic masculinity and creatively builds an alternative, what they see as liberational masculinity. This evaluative structure, while certainly drawing on existing conceptual material, is new in its composite form and is thus a distinct contribution to cultural history and social change.

The men code mainstream masculine identity as constituted in the motivational characteristics of being unreliable, overly rational, close-minded, unimaginative, overly cautious, and disempowered. The social relationships of the hegemonically established male are seen as being emotionally closed off, condemning, suspicious, deceitful, hateful, unloving, overly deferential, and stagnating. Meanwhile, the hegemonic code of social institutions evaluates them as being emotionally dangerous, factional, overly competitive, corrupt, oppressive, and unjust. In this way, the men have taken on a progressive critique: that the dominant institutions in American society are premised on hegemonic masculinity. While progressive feminism forwarded this general idea long before the mythopoetic men's movement, it is an innovation in this specific form. Indeed, it is a significant development that this progressive critique is being championed by men, especially those who are generally quite moderate politically.

To replace what they interpret as hegemonic masculinity, the men of the movement have constructed a liberational code of masculinity as the binary opposite of the hegemonic code. In this vision, the new man is coded as faithful, personal, attentive, communicative, spiritual, open-minded, easy-going, creative, adventurous, direct, and empowered. The social relationships of the liberated male are meant to be emotionally open, supportive, trusting, truthful, intimate, loving, constructively critical, and continuously growing. Meanwhile, men who have freed themselves of hegemonic masculinity are seen as constituting a new form of social institution, one that is emotionally safe, unified, communal, and sacred and marked by freedom, spontaneity, individuality, and a high level of social justice.

The movement is in many ways a resocialization project, bringing together men who are committed to exploring new forms of gender identity and new forms of social interaction. They are actively constructing new identities for themselves as men and presenting their ideas and results to the society at large via face-to-face interaction and popular media coverage. It is reasonable to conclude that the movement's successes in terms of changing gender ideology and the larger culture have had significant effects far beyond the one hundred thousand men who have been directly involved.

The men consistently report that they have been brought out of relative social isolation and into fellowship with other men in the movement. They state that the movement has made them closer emotionally with their partners, brothers, sisters, mothers, fathers, sons, daughters, friends, coworkers, and more. For most participants the movement has increased their emotional awareness and shifted their goals from what they had been socialized into by mainstream society. Men repeatedly credit the movement with helping them take their feelings more seriously and deal with them in nonviolent, non-destructive ways. These are noteworthy changes in men's lives that if multiplied over time may create significant change in the larger society. It can certainly be seen as one contribution to the lessening of larger social problems such as absent and emotionally unavailable fathers and husbands, male sexism, and male violence, including rape and sexual assault.

Branching out from the gender critique, the men of the movement also mobilize a more general vision of social and economic change. They develop a critical understanding of what they see as a dominant culture that focuses too much on material ideals. At times it is even specifically identified as a "capitalist" culture needing major change. The men identify American culture as centered on what they see as a destructive work ethic that drives people to shape their lives around professional success, prestige, and material accumulation. They see this kind of motivational system as excluding, or at least deprioritizing, the pursuit of important values such as love, community, self-development, and spirituality.

An interesting finding with respect to this is that it is not merely a detached critique. In fact, they see themselves as the unwitting agents of this social order. They report that their lives have been largely built around these very ideals and that they have themselves constituted and maintained this system in the past. They are motivated by a sense of anger and betrayal toward the forces through which they have internalized this dominant culture. They see both benefits and costs for the successful participants because they themselves have experienced them. Thus, they speak not in impersonal ways about a system affecting others but in highly specific, emotional ways about a system they feel has deeply limited and damaged their own lives and the lives of everyone with whom they come in contact.

As with the specific critique of hegemonic masculinity, this broader critique is not seen as merely a topic for discursive exploration. Rather, the movement centers on a commitment to creating change in men's lives outside of the mythopoetic context. In some cases men change jobs, alter their career paths, lower their professional goals, and sacrifice money, prestige, and possessions, giving up aspects of the material realm in exchange for advances in the realm of emotions, relationships, and spirituality. They generally report success with this project, identifying the positive changes in their lives and expressing relief at leaving behind much of their previous beliefs and lifestyles.

The men of the movement feel that they must opt out of this dominant set of ideals and create an immediate alternative. However, rather than try to change the larger society through political activism, they choose an unusual individualistic route that is only vaguely aimed at larger social change. While the movement is clearly not going to dramatically alter the larger society, the evidence suggests that it has already contributed to some significant change on the micro level. Any larger historical payoff will likely be the result of the intermingling of these ideas with the contributions of other movements and may be years in the making.

Finally, my empirical research has contributed a deeper understanding of the interactional dynamics of the mythopoetic men's movement, particularly in terms of the small group dynamics of socialization, power, and ideological construction. My research shows the active role of the individual men's group leader in his position as organic intellectual, acting as the interpreter and local practitioner of the high intellectual texts such as those by Robert Bly, James Hillman, and Michael Meade. The leader creatively applies the ideological content of these broader texts, inserting his own cultural interpretations.

The men's group leader uses his local power to exert control and even manipulate men into following his moral and political vision. At the grassroots level, he attempts to create the movement according to his own agenda. He is constrained by the teaching of the high intellectuals, but the empirical evidence suggests that he is much freer in his cultural interpretations than formerly thought. Previous nonethnographic research in the area emphasizing the movement texts has missed the extent to which the actual ideology of the movement is created on the more micro level via the local leaders.

But the power of the organic intellectuals of the movement is far from complete. Men at the local level are actively involved in the process of social construction. Ideas forwarded by group leaders are often contested, negotiated, and reinterpreted. Conceptualizations are always open to questioning and can change over time. Further, the men themselves present new ideas and from time to time wrest control of group processes from the leader. Examining the movement on this detailed level via ethnographic data allows a deeper understanding of how the ideology of the movement is actually developed and applied on the level of lived interaction.

## CULTURAL SOCIOLOGY

This research project pursues several directions of development for the growing field of cultural sociology and cultural analysis more broadly. Specifically, cultural discourse analysis has been used productively in the past on both the theoretical and empirical level, and with this book I attempt to contribute to this larger project. Certainly this new empirical application of the cultural sociology perspective helps to demonstrate its analytical power. However, the present work also expands the perspective, showing that it is effective in handling empirical foci beyond a focus on the discourse of civil society as it has been generally applied.

The application of the lessons of late-Durkheimian work and semiotic approaches via cultural discourse analysis has been extremely effective in uncovering the structured meanings that animate the mythopoetic movement. Without such a theoretical apparatus, understanding of the cultural dimension of the movement would be deeply limited. Motivation and ideological content could not be understood in as much depth without the use of carefully constructed cultural tools. Indeed, the data show empirically that the discourse of the movement is structured in oppositional, binary ways as shown through years of close ethnographic research. The movement participants evaluate the social world in terms of sacred and profane codes that then direct and motivate their actions within the movement contexts and beyond.

One major innovation of the current research has been the attempt to show that issues of power, hegemony, social control, and social change can be addressed via work that is fully cultural and thus is not hampered by the pitfalls of traditional Marxist, materialist analysis. Taking some steps in this direction, my analysis adapts the Gramscian concept of hegemony and his theoretical system dealing with organic and high intellectuals.

My analysis takes an inductive approach with respect to power rather than assuming its constitutive role. Thus this project cannot claim to have discovered objective hegemonic masculinity; rather, it has uncovered one major understanding of hegemonic masculinity. My approach is true to the social constructionist premise that a social phenomenon is real if it is real in its consequences. With respect to the mythopoetic men's movement specifically, if significant numbers of individuals understand there to be a hegemonic masculinity and react in a meaningful, organized way against it, then there will be a relevant outcome. In this case, then, history is not being made by power itself in a materialist way but instead by individuals acting according to cultural notions of power.

I adapt the Gramscian system of high and organic intellectuals as part of a larger cultural approach. Examining the dynamics empirically, my analysis shows that the role of the mythopoetic men's leader can be more deeply understood through the use of a cultural version of the organic intellectual conceptualization. The leader takes on a powerful role in interaction through the utilization of the texts and overall authority of the high intellectuals of the movement. In the institution of the men's group, the data show that the leader takes on the role of socialization agent through his place in the cultural system of movement intellectuals. He is understood by group members as "one of them" at the same time that he is a conduit for higher movement ideals, and therefore the conceptualizations he forwards are more likely to be believed and acted upon.

This approach does not suppose the objective truth of the teachings of organic intellectuals, as in Marxist analysis. Rather, the ideals espoused are simply another form of ideology, in the Geertzian sense, and have causal power only when empirically shown to do so. The leader is accorded power according to his corresponding status in the counterhegemonic movement primarily because of the belief in his power on the part of the individual members. Participants create and support the authority of the leader through their belief in his cultural conceptualizations. They constitute his power culturally, not solely via objective characteristics of material reality. I show this in this study inductively through ethnographic data.

Hegemony is seen here as power that must be legitimized and can only be authoritative through microcultural interpretive techniques. All cultural life can be seen as filled with the exercise of power, which is generated inside the local meaning system but also draws from larger cultural and material sources. Thus hegemony and power can be the result of using cultural codes for a certain social outcome. In cultural Marxist terms, discourse constitutes power. However, avoiding the trap of orthodox materialism, discourse can be understood as the result of creative individuals making cultural ideas. These ideas, here in the form of cultural discourses, then act back upon individuals by motivating action. Here, power is morally and politically neutral; it can be used to support inequality and existing social relations at the same time it can be used to drive progressive, counterhegemonic social movements. This perspective helps to develop cultural sociology by beginning to address the repeated critique that cultural work does not or cannot incorporate power.

## INTERACTION, ETHNOGRAPHY, AND MICROSOCIOLOGY

Another area in which this study contributes is that of interactional analysis, ethnography, and microsociology in general. The various sub-fields within microsociology have always had as one of their strengths the ability to robustly understand the dynamics of interaction, individual agency, and contingency. Macrosociology has always been limited by its lack of appreciation of the microlevel social world that ultimately constitutes every dynamic studied by macrolevel analysis. Likewise, microsociology has been limited by its circumscribed recognition of the macrodynamics that have significant causal effects on individual action. This project presents an example of how microlevel interaction can be studied, using ethnographic methods, in ways that begin to appreciate the effects of larger scale social dynamics including culture and power. This is something that has only rarely been done within the tradition of ethnographic research. Additionally, this is a contribution to the Alexander tradition of cultural sociology, which has almost always used written texts as its empirical sources.

The research method employed here of multiyear, longitudinal ethnography shows that the men of the mythopoetic men's movement are actively involved in creating the cultural ideas that guide the movement. They come together and create new ways to understand the social world, developing critical conceptualizations that, while not entirely new, are ultimately a new crystallization that they are inserting into society in their local moment of history. It is a creative process that is undergone meeting after meeting, week after week, in face-to-face, relatively spontaneous interaction.

This creative work is not random and unstructured. In fact, the men of the mythopoetic men's movement are working within the framework of an ideology that preceded them in a related form and that is informed by the larger culture, including the texts produced by the high intellectuals of the movement. Each of them joined the preexisting mythopoetic men's movement and proceeded from that point. Each individual then made his own contributions and the movement grew and developed over time because of these many small individual actions. Indeed, in one sense there is no movement beyond its individual members. At the same time, there is a product of their collective interaction. There is a direction to the movement, including the reformation of hegemonic masculinity and the change in beliefs about work and material achievement.

The appreciation of the role of the men's group leader as an organic intellectual has helped in understanding ways in which an individual can act creatively while simultaneously acting in certain culturally structured ways in relation to a larger social system. The men's group leader is an individual who has his own creative interpretations of the larger world and of the issues central to the mythopoetic movement. The men's groups that he leads and the other mythopoetic events in which he is involved show the direct effects of his individual contributions. Nonetheless, he is also in part a product of the very movement that he helps constitute. He interprets a structured set of ideas handed down to him by the movement high intellectuals. Further, his actions are the product of interaction with the rank-and-file movement members, who each have their own ideas and interpretations with which they are ready to contest his cultural authority. Ultimately the current cultural discourse of the movement at any one moment is a collective product of the continuous ongoing interactions of everyone involved. While some individuals have more power in the development of this cultural discourse, no individual has total power and no individual is completely powerless. Relatedly, the social dynamics are always open to individual agency, and no actor is ever a culturally programmed "judgmental dope."

In conclusion, it has been possible to develop deeper understandings of both the interaction within the mythopoetic men's movement and the larger cultural discourse/political ideology of the movement by studying both simultaneously. A broader suggestion is that individual action can only be fully understood when it is linked theoretically and empirically to issues of culture and power. Cultural analysis can be further developed by the inclusion of the appreciation of interaction and agency as well as the dynamics of power and hegemony; and simultaneously, work interested in the area of power, social movements, and social change can be furthered through the robust appreciation of culture and of microlevel dynamics. While these potential achievements are far from being fully accomplished in the social sciences, this project has aimed to make a small contribution to their continuing development.

# References

Adorno, Theodor W., Else Frenkel-Brunswick, Daniel J. Levinson, and R. Nevitt Sanford. 1950. *The Authoritarian Personality.* New York: Harper.

Alexander, Jeffrey. 1992. "Citizen and Enemy as Symbolic Classification: On the Polarizing Discourse of Civil Society." In *Where Culture Talks: Exclusion and the Making of Society,* ed. Marcel Fournier and Michele Lamont, 289–308. Chicago: University of Chicago Press.

———. 2003. *The Meanings of Social Life: A Cultural Sociology.* New York: Oxford University Press.

———. 2006. *The Civil Sphere.* New York: Oxford University Press.

Alexander, Jeffrey C., and Steven Seidman, eds. 1990. *Culture and Society: Contemporary Debates.* Cambridge: Cambridge University Press.

Alexander, Jeffrey C., and Philip Smith. 1993. "The Discourse of American Civil Society: A New Proposal for Cultural Studies." *Theory and Society* 22:151–207.

Asch, S. E. 1956. "Studies of Independence and Conformity: A Minority of One against a Unanimous Majority." *Psychological Monographs: General and Applied* 70:1–70.

Bartkowski, J. P. 2000. "Breaking Walls, Raising Fences: Masculinity, Intimacy, and Accountability among the Promise Keepers." *Sociology of Religion* 61:33–53.

———. 2002. "Godly Masculinities: Gender Discourse among the Promise Keepers." *Social Thought and Research* 24:53–87.

———. 2003. *The Promise Keepers: Servants, Soldiers, and Godly Men.* New Brunswick, N.J.: Rutgers University Press.

Barton, Edward Read, ed. 2000. *Mythopoetic Perspectives of Men's Healing Work: An Anthology for Therapists and Others.* Westport, Conn.: Bergin and Garvey.

Beck, Charlotte Joko. 1993. *Nothing Special: Living Zen.* New York: Harper-Collins.

Bednarik, Karl. 1970. *The Male in Crisis.* Trans. Helen Sebba. New York: Knopf.

Bly, Robert. 1990. *Iron John: A Book about Men.* Reading, Mass.: Addison-Wesley.

Bly, Robert, James Hillman, and Michael Meade, eds. 1992. *The Rag and Bone Shop of the Heart: Poems for Men.* New York: HarperCollins.

Boehm, Felix. 1930. "The Femininity Complex in Men." *International Journal of Psycho-Analysis* 11:444–69.

Bourdieu, Pierre. 1984. *Distinction: A Social Critique of the Judgment of Taste.* London: Routledge and Kegan Paul.

Braaten, L. J. 1991. "Group Cohesion: A New Multidimensional Model." *Group* 15:39–55.

Brannon, Robert. 1976. "The Male Sex Role: Our Culture's Blueprint of Manhood and What It's Done for Us Lately." In *The Forty-Nine Percent Majority: The Male Sex Role,* ed. Deborah S. David and Robert Brannon, 1–45. Reading, Mass.: Addison-Wesley.

Brehmer, B. 1976. "Social Judgment Theory and the Analysis of Interpersonal Conflict." *Psychological Bulletin* 83:985–1003.

Brittan, Arthur. 1989. *Masculinity and Power.* Oxford, U.K.: Blackwell.

Carrigan, Tim, R .W. Connell, and John Lee. 1985. "Toward a New Sociology of Masculinity." *Theory and Society* 14:551–604.

Carron, A. V. 1982. "Cohesiveness in Sports Teams: Implications and Considerations." *Journal of Sports Psychology* 4:123–38.

Chapple, Steve, and David Talbot. 1990. *Burning Desires: Sex in America.* New York: Simon and Schuster.

Chodorow, Nancy. 1978. *The Reproduction of Mothering: Psychoanalysis and the Sociology of Gender.* Berkeley: University of California Press.

———. 1985. "Beyond Drive Theory: Object Relations and the Limits of Radical Individualism." *Theory and Society* 14:271–319.

Clatterbaugh, Kenneth C. 1997. *Contemporary Perspectives on Masculinity: Men, Women, and Politics in Modern Society.* Boulder, Colo.: Westview Press.

Cockburn, Cynthia. 1983. *Brothers: Male Dominance and Technological Change.* London: Pluto Press.

———. 1991. *In the Way of Women: Men's Resistance to Sex Equality in Organizations.* London: Macmillan.

Collins, Randall. 1989. "The Durkheimian Tradition in Conflict Sociology." In *Durkheimian Sociology: Cultural Studies,* ed. Jeffrey Alexander, 107–28. Berkeley: University of California Press.

Collinson, David, David Knights, and Margaret Collinson. 1990. *Managing to Discriminate.* London: Routledge.

Connell, R. W. 1979. "The Concept of 'Role' and What to Do with It." *Australian and New Zealand Journal of Sociology* 15:7–17.

———. 1989. "Cool Guys, Swots, and Wimps: The Interplay of Masculinity and Education." *Oxford Review of Education* 15:291–303.

———. 1995. *Masculinities.* Berkeley: University of California Press.

———. 2005. *Masculinities.* 2nd ed. Berkeley: University of California Press.

Corman, June, Meg Luxton, David Livingstone, and Wally Seccombe. 1993. *Recasting Steel Labour: The Stelco Story.* Halifax, N.S.: Fernwood.

Deutsch, Morton. 1973. *The Resolution of Conflict: Constructive and Destructive Processes.* New Haven, Conn.: Yale University Press.

DiMaggio, Paul, and Walter Powell. 1983. "The Iron Cage Revisited: Institutional Isomorphism and Collective Rationality in Organization Fields." *American Sociological Review* 48:147–60.

Dinnerstein, Dorothy. 1976. *The Mermaid and the Minotaur: Sexual Arrangements and Human Malaise.* New York: Harper and Row.

Donaldson, Mike. 1991. *Time of Our Lives: Labour and Love in the Working Class.* Sydney: Allen and Unwin.

Douglas, Mary. 1966. *Purity and Danger: An Analysis of Concepts of Pollution and Taboo.* London: Penguin.

Durkheim, Émile. 1961. *The Elementary Forms of the Religious Life.* Trans. Joseph Ward Swain. New York: Collier Books.

Edles, Laura. 1998. *Symbol and Ritual in the New Spain: The Transition to Democracy after Franco.* Cambridge: Cambridge University Press.

Eisler, Riane. 1992. "What Do Men Really Want? The Men's Movement, Partnership, and Domination." In *Women Respond to the Men's Movement: A Feminist Collection,* ed. Kay Leigh Hagan, 43–54. San Francisco: HarperCollins.

Eliade, Mircea. 1957. *The Sacred and the Profane: The Nature of Religion.* New York: Harper.

Eliasoph, Nina. 1990. "Political Culture and the Presentation of a Political 'Self.'" *Theory and Society* 19:465–94.

———. 1998. *Avoiding Politics: How Americans Produce Apathy in Everyday Life.* New York: Cambridge University Press.

———. 2002. "Raising Good Citizens in a Bad Society: Moral Education and Political Avoidance in Civic America." In *Meaning and Modernity: Religion, Polity, Self,* ed. Richard Madsen, William M. Sullivan, Ann Swidler, and Steven M. Tipton, 195–223. Berkeley: University of California Press.

Eliasoph, Nina, and Paul Lichterman. 2003. "Culture in Interaction." *American Journal of Sociology* 108:735–94.

Evans, N. J., and P. A. Jarvis. 1980. "Group Cohesion: A Review and Reevaluation." *Small Group Behavior* 11:359–70.

Fantasia, Rick. 1988. *Cultures of Solidarity: Consciousness, Action, and Contemporary American Workers.* Berkeley: University of California Press.

Ferber, A. L. 2000. "Racial Warriors and Weekend Warriors: The Construction of Masculinity in Mythopoetic and White Supremacist Discourse." *Men and Masculinities* 3:30–56.

Fields, Rick, ed. 1994. *The Awakened Warrior: Living with Courage, Compassion, and Discipline.* New York: Putnam.

Fodor, E. M., and T. Smith. 1982. "The Power Motive as an Influence on Group Decision Making." *Journal of Personality and Social Psychology* 42:178–85.

Fox, J. 2004. "How Men's Movement Participants View Each Other." *Journal of Men's Studies* 12:103–18.

Fromm, Erich. 1942. *The Fear of Freedom.* London: Routledge and Kegan Paul.

Garfinkel, Harold. 1967. *Studies in Ethnomethodology.* Englewood Cliffs, N.J.: Prentice Hall.

Garrison, Dee. 1981. "Karen Horney and Feminism." *Signs* 6:672–91.

Geertz, Clifford. 1973. *The Interpretation of Cultures.* New York: Basic.

Gilligan, Carol. 1982. *In a Different Voice: Psychological Theory and Women's Development.* Cambridge, Mass.: Harvard University Press.

Goffman, Erving. 1970. *Asylums: Essays on the Social Situation of Mental Patients and Other Inmates.* Chicago: Aldine.

———.1973. *The Presentation of Self in Everyday Life.* Woodstock, N.Y.: Overlook Press.

Gramsci, Antonio. 1971. *Selections from the Prison Notebooks.* Ed. and trans. Quintin Hoare and Geoffrey Nowell Smith. New York: International Publishers.

Grazian, David. 2003. *Blue Chicago: The Search for Authenticity in Urban Blues Clubs.* Chicago: University of Chicago Press.

———. 2004. "The Production of Popular Music as a Confidence Game: The Case of the Chicago Blues." *Qualitative Sociology* 27:137–58.

Grindstaff, Laura. 2002. *The Money Shot: Trash, Class, and the Making of TV Talk Shows.* Chicago: University of Chicago Press.

Grosz, Elizabeth A. 1990. *Jacques Lacan: A Feminist Introduction.* London: Routledge.

Gruneau, Richard, and David Whitson. 1993. *Hockey Night in Canada: Sport, Identities, and Cultural Politics.* Toronto: Garamond Press.

Habermas, Jürgen. 1984. *The Theory of Communicative Action, Vol 1: Reason and the Rationalization of Society.* Boston: Beacon Press.

———. 1987. *The Theory of Communicative Action, Vol 2: Lifeworld and System: A Critique of Functionalist Reason.* Boston: Beacon Press.

Hacker, Helen M. 1957. "The New Burdens of Masculinity." *Marriage and Family Living* 19:227–33.

Hagan, Kay Leigh, ed. 1992. *Women Respond to the Men's Movement: A Feminist Collection.* San Francisco: HarperCollins.

Hall, Stuart, and Martin Jacques, eds. 1989. *New Times: The Changing Face of Politics in the 1990s.* London: Lawrence and Wishart.

Hall, Stuart, and Tony Jefferson. 1989. *Resistance through Rituals: Youth Subcultures in Postwar Britain.* London: Unwin Hyman.

Hartley, Ruth E. 1959. "Sex Role Pressures in the Socialization of the Male Child." *Psychological Reports* 5:457–68.

Hastie, R. 1986. "Review Essay: Experimental Evidence on Group Accuracy." In *Information Pooling and Group Decision Making: Proceedings of the Second University of California, Irvine, Conference on Political Economy,* ed. Bernard Grofman and Guillermo Owen, 129–57. New York: Grune and Stratton.

Hays, Kim. 1994. *Practicing Virtues: Moral Traditions at Quaker and Military Boarding Schools.* Berkeley: University of California Press.

Hearn, Jeff. 1987. *The Gender of Oppression: Men, Masculinity, and the Critique of Marxism.* Brighton, U.K.: Wheatsheaf.

Hearn, Jeff, and David Morgan, eds. 1990. *Men, Masculinities, and Social Theory.* London: Unwin Hyman.

Hearn, Jeff, and Wendy Parkin. 2001. *Gender, Sexuality, and Violence in Organizations: The Unspoken Forces of Organization Violations.* Thousand Oaks, Calif.: Sage.

Hebdige, Dick. 1979. *Subculture: The Meaning of Style.* London: Methuen.

Hillman, James. 1989. *A Blue Fire: Selected Writings.* New York: Harper and Row.

Horkheimer, Max, ed. 1936. *Studien uber Autoritat und Familie.* Paris: Alcan.

Horney, Karen. 1932. "The Dread of Woman: Observations on a Specific Difference in the Dread Felt by Men and by Women Respectively for the Opposite Sex." *International Journal of Psycho-Analysis* 13:348–60.

Irigaray, Luce. 1985. *This Sex Which Is Not One.* Ithaca, N.Y.: Cornell University Press.

Jacobs, Ronald N. 1996. "Civil Society and Crisis: Culture, Discourse, and the Rodney King Beating." *American Journal of Sociology* 101 (5): 1238–72.

———. 1998. "The Racial Discourse of Civil Society." In *Real Civil Societies: The Dilemmas of Institutionalization,* ed. Jeffrey Alexander, 138–61. Newbury Park, Calif.: Sage.

Jacoby, Russell. 1975. *Social Amnesia: A Critique of Conformist Psychology from Adler to Laing.* Boston: Beacon Press.

Janis, Irving L. 1982. *Groupthink: Psychological Studies of Policy Decisions and Fiascoes.* 2nd ed. Boston: Houghton Mifflin.

Kane, Anne. 1991. "Cultural Analysis in Historical Sociology: The Concrete and Analytic Autonomy of Culture." *Sociological Theory* 9:53–69.

———. 1997. "Theorizing Meaning Construction in Social Movements: Symbolic Structures and Interpretation during the Irish Land War, 1879–1882." *Sociological Theory* 15 (3): 249–76.

Karides, M. 1998. "Writing about Men: Mythopoets and Qualitative Researchers." *Qualitative Sociology* 21:205–9.

Kauth, Bill. 1992. *A Circle of Men: The Original Manual for Men's Support Groups.* New York: St. Martin's.

Keen, Sam. 1989. *Your Mythic Journey: Finding Meaning in Your Life through Writing and Storytelling.* New York: St. Martin's.

———. 1991. *Fire in the Belly: On Being a Man.* New York: Bantam.

Kessler, Suzanne J., and Wendy McKenna. 1978. *Gender: An Ethnomethodological Approach.* New York: Wiley.

Kimmel, Michael S. 1987. "Rethinking Masculinity: New Directions in Research." In *Changing Men: New Directions in Research on Men and Masculinity,* ed. Michael S. Kimmel, 9–24. Newbury Park, Calif.: Sage.

———. 1996. *Manhood in America: A Cultural History.* New York: Free Press.

Kimmel, Michael S., and Michael Kaufman. 1994. "Weekend Warriors: The New Men's Movement." In *Theorizing Masculinities,* ed. Harry Brod and Michael Kaufman, 259–88. London: Sage.

Klein, Alan M. 1993. *Little Big Men: Bodybuilding Subculture and Gender Construction.* Albany: State University of New York Press.

Klein, Melanie. 1928. "Early Stages of the Oedipus Conflict." *International Journal of Psycho-Analysis* 9:167–80.

Komarovsky, Mirra. 1946. "Cultural Contradictions of Sex Roles." *American Journal of Sociology* 52:184–89.

———. 1950. "Functional Analysis of Sex Roles." *American Sociological Review* 15:508–16.

Kornfield, Jack. 1993. *A Path with Heart: A Guide through the Perils and Promises of Spiritual Life.* New York: Bantam.

———. 1994. *Buddha's Little Instruction Book.* New York: Bantam.

Lamont, M. 1992. *Money, Morals and Manners: The Culture of the French and American Upper Middle Class.* Chicago: University of Chicago Press.

———. 2000. *The Dignity of Working Men: Morality and the Boundaries of Race, Class, and Immigration.* Cambridge, Mass.: Harvard University Press.

Lawler, Edward J. 1992. "Power Process in Bargaining." *Sociological Quarterly* 33:17–34.

Lawler, Edward J., and Rebecca Ford. 1995. "Bargaining and Influence in Conflict Situations." In *Sociological Perspectives on Social Psychology,* ed. Karen S. Cook, Gary Alan Fine, and James S. House, 236–56. Needham Heights, Mass.: Allyn and Bacon.

Leana, C. R. 1985. "A Partial Test of Janis' Groupthink Model: Effects of Group Cohesiveness and Leader Behavior on Defective Decision Making." *Journal of Management* 11:5–17.

Lichterman, P. 1995. "Piecing Together Multicultural Community: Cultural Differences in Community Building among Grassroots Environmentalists." *Social Problems* 42:13–34.

———. 1996. *The Search for Political Community: American Activists Reinventing Commitment.* New York: Cambridge University Press.

———. 1998. "What Do Movements Mean? The Value of Participant Observation." *Qualitative Sociology* 21:401–18.

———. 1999. "Talking Identity in the Public Sphere: Broad Visions and Small Spaces in Sexual Identity Politics." *Theory and Society* 28:101–41.

———. 2002. "Seeing Structure Happen: Theory-Driven Participant Observation." In *Methods of Social Movement Research,* ed. Bert Klandermans and Suzanne Staggenborg, 118–45. Minneapolis: University of Minnesota Press.

———. 2005. *Elusive Togetherness: Religious Groups and Civic Engagement in America.* Princeton, N.J.: Princeton University Press.

Magnuson, Eric. 1997. "Ideological Conflict in American Political Culture: The Discourse of Civil Society and American National Narratives in

American History Textbooks." *International Journal of Sociology and Social Policy* 17 (6): 84–130.

———. 2005. "Cultural Discourse in Action: Interactional Dynamics and Symbolic Meaning." *Qualitative Sociology* 28: 371–98.

———. 2007. "Creating Culture in the Mythopoetic Men's Movement: An Ethnographic Study of Micro-level Leadership and Socialization." *Journal of Men's Studies* 15: 31–56.

———. Forthcoming. "Rejecting the American Dream: Men Creating Alternative Life Goals." *Journal of Contemporary Ethnography.*

McKay, Jim, Michael A. Messner, and Don Sabo, eds. 2000. *Masculinities, Gender Relations, and Sport.* Thousand Oaks, Calif.: Sage.

Meade, Michael. 1993. *Men and the Water of Life: Initiation and the Tempering of Men.* San Francisco: HarperCollins.

Messner, Michael. 1992. *Power at Play: Sports and the Problem of Masculinity.* Boston: Beacon.

———. 1997. *Politics of Masculinities: Men in Movements.* Thousand Oaks, Calif.: Sage.

———. 2000. "Barbie Girls versus Sea Monsters: Children Constructing Gender." *Gender and Society* 14 (6): 765–84.

———. 2002. *Taking the Field: Women, Men, and Sports.* Minneapolis: University of Minnesota Press.

Messner, Michael, and Don Sabo, eds. 1990. *Sport, Men, and the Gender Order: Critical Feminist Perspectives.* Champaign, Ill.: Human Kinetics.

———. 1994. *Sex, Violence, and Power in Sports: Rethinking Masculinity.* Freedom, Calif.: Crossing Press.

Michener, H. Andrew, and Michelle P. Wasserman. 1995. "Group Decision Making." In *Sociological Perspectives on Social Psychology,* ed. Karen S. Cook, Gary Alan Fine, and James S. House, 335–61. Needham Heights, Mass.: Allyn and Bacon.

Mitchell, Juliet. 1975. *Psychoanalysis and Feminism.* New York: Vintage.

Mood, John J. L. 1975. *Rilke on Love and Other Difficulties: Translations and Considerations of Rainer Maria Rilke.* New York: Norton.

Moore, Robert L., and Douglas Gillette. 1990. *King, Warrior, Magician, Lover: Rediscovering the Archetypes of the Mature Masculine.* San Francisco: HarperCollins.

Moore, Thomas. 1994. *Soul Mates: Honoring the Mysteries of Love and Relationships.* New York: HarperCollins.

Moorhead, G., and J. R. Montanari. 1986. "An Empirical Investigation of the Groupthink Phenomenon." *Human Relations* 39:399–410.

Morgan, David. 1981. "Men, Masculinity, and the Process of Sociological Inquiry." In *Doing Feminist Research,* ed. Helen Roberts, 83–113. London: Routledge and Kegan Paul.

Mudrack, P. E. 1989. "Defining Group Cohesiveness: A Legacy of Confusion?" *Small Group Behavior* 20:37–49.

Newton, J. 2005. *From Panthers to Promise Keepers: Rethinking the Men's Movement.* Lanham, MD: Rowman and Littlefield.

Ortner, Sherry. 1974. "Is Female to Male as Nature Is to Culture?" In *Woman, Culture, and Society*, ed. Michelle Zimbalist Rosaldo and Louise Lamphere, 67–87. Palo Alto, Calif.: Stanford University Press.

Parsons, Talcott. 1964a. "Age and Sex in the Social Structure of the United States." In *Essays in Sociological Theory*. New York: Free Press.

———. 1964b. "The Kinship System of the Contemporary United States." In *Essays in Sociological Theory*. New York: Free Press.

Parsons, Talcott, and Robert F. Bales. 1956. *Family, Socialization, and Interaction Process*. London: Routledge and Kegan Paul.

Pleck, Joseph H. 1976. "The Male Sex Role: Definitions, Problems, and Sources of Change." *Journal of Social Issues* 32:155–64.

———. 1981. *The Myth of Masculinity*. Cambridge, Mass.: MIT Press.

Pye, Lucien. 1988. *The Mandarin and the Cadre: China's Political Cultures*. Ann Arbor: University of Michigan Press.

Rabinovitch, Eyal. 2001. "Gender and the Public Sphere: Alternative Forms of Integration in Nineteenth-century America." *Sociological Theory* 19: 344–70.

Reich, Wilhelm. 1970. *The Mass Psychology of Fascism*. Trans. Vincent R. Carfagno. New York: Farrar, Strauss, and Giroux.

———. 1972. *Sex-pol: Essays, 1929–1934*. New York: Vintage.

Richard-Allerdyce, Diane. 1994. "Hearing the Other: Social Change and Individual Growth in Women's, Men's, and Eco-Spirituality Movements." *Feminist Issues* 14 (1): 57–67.

Riesman, David. 1953. *The Lonely Crowd: A Study of the Changing American Character*. Garden City, N.J.: Doubleday Anchor.

Roudinesco, Elisabeth. 1990. *Jacques Lacan and Co.: A History of Psychoanalysis in France, 1925–1985*. Chicago: University of Chicago Press.

Rowbotham, Sheila. 1981. "The Women's Movement and Organizing for Socialism." In *Beyond the Fragments: Feminism and the Making of Socialism*, ed. Sheila Rowbotham, Lynne Segal, and Hilary Wainwright, 121–55. Boston: Alyson Publications.

———. 1989. *The Past Is before Us: Feminism in Action since the 1960s*. Boston: Beacon.

Rubin, Gayle. 1975. "The Traffic in Women: Notes on the Political Economy of Sex." In *Toward an Anthropology of Women*, ed. Rayna Reiter, 157–210. New York: Monthly Review Press.

Saussure, Ferdinand de. 1985. "The Linguistic Sign." In *Semiotics: An Introductory Anthology*, ed. Robert E. Innis, 28–46. Bloomington: Indiana University Press.

Schelling, Thomas C. 1960. *The Strategy of Conflict*. New York: Oxford University Press.

Schwalbe, Michael. 1995. "Mythopoetic Men's Work as a Search for Communitas." In *Men's Lives*, 3rd ed., ed. Michael S. Kimmel and Michael A. Messner, 507–19. Boston: Allyn and Bacon.

———. 1996. *Unlocking the Iron Cage: The Men's Movement, Gender Politics, and American Culture*. New York: Oxford University Press.

Segal, Lynne. 1990. *Slow Motion: Changing Masculinities, Changing Men.* London: Virago.

———. 1999. *Why Feminism? Gender, Psychology, Politics.* New York: Columbia University Press.

Seidler, Victor J. 1986. *Kant, Respect, and Injustice: The Limits of Liberal Moral Theory.* Boston: Routledge and Kegan Paul.

———. 1989. *Rediscovering Masculinity: Reason, Language, and Sexuality.* London: Routledge.

———. 1991. *Recreating Sexual Politics: Men, Feminism, and Politics.* London: Routledge.

Sewell, William. 1992. "Narratives and Social Identities." *Social Science History* 16 (3): 479–88.

Sexton, Patricia Cayo. 1969. *The Feminized Male: Classrooms, White Collars, and the Decline of Manliness.* New York: Random House.

Sherwood, Steven Jay. 1994. "Narrating the Social: Postmodernism and the Drama of Democracy." *Journal of Narrative and Life History* 4 (1–2): 69–88.

Shils, Edward. 1975. *Center and Periphery: Essays in Macrosociology.* Chicago: University of Chicago Press.

Smith, Philip. 1991. "Codes and Conflict: Toward a Theory of War as Ritual." *Theory and Society* 20 (1): 103–38.

———. 1994. "The Semiotics of Media Narratives: Saddam and Nasser in the American Mass Media." *Journal of Narrative and Life History* 4 (1–2): 89–118.

———. 1996. "Executing Executions: Aesthetics, Identity, and the Problematic Narratives of Capital Punishment Ritual." *Theory and Society* 25 (2): 235–61.

———. 1998. "Communism, Fascism, and Democracy: Barbarism and Civility as Variations on a Common Theme." In *Real Civil Societies: The Dilemmas of Institutionalization,* ed. Jeffrey Alexander, 115–37. Newbury Park, Calif.: Sage.

Somers, Margaret. 1992. "Narrativity, Narrative Identity, and Social Action: Rethinking English Working Class Formation." *Social Science History* 16 (4): 591–630.

Somers, Margaret, and Gloria Gibson. 1993. "Reclaiming the Epistemological 'Other': Narrative and the Social Constitution of Identity." In *From Persons to Nations: The Social Constitution of Identities,* ed. Craig Calhoun. London: Basil Blackwell.

Stacey, Judith, and Barrie Thorne. 1985. "The Missing Feminist Revolution in Sociology." *Social Problems* 32:301–16.

Stallybrass, Peter, and Allan Whyte. 1986. *The Politics and Poetics of Transgression.* Ithaca, N.Y.: Cornell University Press.

Steinem, Gloria. 1992. "Foreword." In *Women Respond to the Men's Movement: A Feminist Collection,* ed. Kay Leigh Hagan, vii–xii. San Francisco: HarperCollins.

Strathern, Marilyn. 1980. "No Nature, No Culture: The Hagen Case." In

*Nature, Culture and Gender,* eds. Carol P. MacCormack and Marilyn Strathern, 174–222. Cambridge: Cambridge University Press.

Suzuki, Shunryu. 1993. *Zen Mind, Beginner's Mind: Informal Talks on Zen Meditation and Practice.* New York: Weatherhill.

Swidler, A. 2001. *Talk of Love: How Culture Matters.* Chicago: University of Chicago Press.

Tedeschi, James T., Barry R. Schlenker, and Thomas V. Bonoma. 1973. *Conflict, Power, and Games: The Experimental Study of Interpersonal Relations.* Chicago: Aldine.

Trungpa, Chogyam. 1984. *Shambala: The Sacred Path of the Warrior.* New York: Random House.

Turner, Victor. 1969. *The Ritual Process.* Chicago: Aldine.

Wagner-Pacifici, Robin. 1994. *Discourse and Destruction: The City of Philadelphia versus MOVE.* Chicago: University of Chicago Press.

Weber, Max. 1992. *The Protestant Ethic and the Spirit of Capitalism.* New York: Routledge.

West, Brad, and Philip Smith. 1996. "Drought, Discourse, and Durkheim." *Australian and New Zealand Journal of Sociology* 32(1): 93–102.

———. 1997. "Natural Disasters and National Identity: Time, Space, and Mythology." *Australian and New Zealand Journal of Sociology* 33 (2): 205–15.

Williamson, Gay. 1994. "Transformative Ritual." In *Transformative Rituals: Celebrations for Personal Growth,* ed. Gay Williamson and David Williamson, 57. New York: HCI Books.

Willis, Paul. 1977. *Learning to Labor: How Working-Class Kids Get Working-Class Jobs.* London: Saxon House Books.

Wrong, Dennis. 1961. "The Over-Socialized Conception of Man in Modern Sociology." *American Sociological Review* 26:183–93.

Wuthnow, Robert. 1987. *Meaning and Moral Order: Explorations in Cultural Analysis.* Berkeley: University of California Press.

# Index

Adorno, Theodor, 26
Alexander, Jeffrey, 11, 79–80
American work ethic, 10–11, 102, 103–104, 147; critique of, 112–113, 139–140; and drive to achieve, 108, 109, 142n.; and dysfunction, 107; effect on members of men's movement, 103, 104–108, 118–121; elusiveness of success, 111–112; emotional damage caused by, 106–109, 112; and organizational structures, 127; work as avoidance, 110; workplace values colonizing personal life, 132–135. *See also* Mythopoetic ethic
Androgyny, 3

Biological materialism, 24, 25
Bly, Robert, 1; as high intellectual of movement, 46, 57; on importance of groups, 53; and influence of Jung, 25; theoretical shortcomings of, 25–26, 35; writing method, 91–92. *See also Iron John*; *The Rag and Bone Shop of the Heart*

Capitalism, 147; and organizational structures, 127; resistance to, 88–89, 127–128. *See also The Protestant Ethic and the Spirit of Capitalism*
Chodorow, Nancy, 26–27
*A Circle of Men*, 57
Conflict resolution, 94–96

Consciousness-raising, 4; personal experience as social phenomenon, 44–45; role of organic intellectuals, 45–48; and social change, 44–45
Counterhegemonic masculinity. *See* Mythopoetic masculinity
Cultural discourse, 76–77, 97, 143, 144–145; Alexanderian approach, 11, 79–80; common cultural space for interaction, 81–84; construction of mythopoetic masculinity, 91–92; critical alternative to mainstream culture, 84–91, 99n.; and cultural-ideological conflict, 78; as evaluative process, 77–78; internalizing and externalizing cultural components, 78–79, 99n.; of mythopoetic men's movement, 80, 97, 98t.; presence in all social action, 78; structure and microstructures of culture, 77. *See also* Mythopoetic ethic
"Cultural dope," 99n.
Cultural sociology, 11–12, 143, 149–150; application to gender and masculinity studies, 21; and ethnography, 12; idealism versus reductionism, 75–76. *See also* Microsociology; Social sciences
Culture, defined, 77

Dinnerstein, Dorothy, 26–27
Durkheim, Émile, 17, 149; and "sex role" framework, 27

163

changes in personal lives, 113–118; check-ins, 52, 56, 92; conflict resolution, 94–96; David's life change, 127–130; Dennis's life change, 126–127; and dramatic life changes, 117–127, 140; Henry's life change, 136–139; Kevin's life change, 125–126; meeting format, 51–53; Nick's life change, 130–136, 142n.; and personal growth, 96–97; and political issues, 88–90, 99n.; power dynamics, 62–63, 66, 67–68; prohibition against shaming, 91, 93–94; proscription against idea of inability to change, 115–116; resistance to capitalism, 88–89, 127–128; ritual objects, 51; Sam's life change, 121–123; and smaller movement-inspired changes, 118, 127–139, 140–141; as supportive community, 81–84, 99n.; Terrence's life change, 123–125; Watani as socializing agent, 46, 62–63. *See also* Socialization; Watani

Organic intellectuals, 9, 11–12, 144, 148, 151–152; competition between, 73n.; and identification of hegemonic ideology, 47–48; as links between high intellectuals and population at large, 46–47; and socialization process, 48, 73. *See also* High intellectuals; Socialization; Watani

Parsons, Talcott, 17, 27
*A Path with Heart*, 59
Personal growth, 96–97
Personal responsibility, 107–108, 110–111, 129–130, 142n.
Physical aggression, 91, 93
Poetry and stories, 58–60, 91–92; telling one's story for the last time, 115
Popular texts, and scholarly analysis, 35–36
Promotional leadership, 49–50
Proposition 187 (California), 62

*The Protestant Ethic and the Spirit of Capitalism*, 103–104
Psychological/Freudian paradigm, 21, 24–27, 39, 40n.
Pyramid organizational structure, 127

*The Rag and Bone Shop of the Heart*, 59, 92
Reich, Wilhelm, 26, 40n.
Richard-Allerdyce, Diane, 38
Role conflict, 29

Schwalbe, Michael, 36–37
Sex, defined, 22
Sex role/functionalist paradigm, 21, 27–30, 39
Shaming, 91, 93–94
Social change: and consciousness-raising, 44–45; and gender crisis, 2, 6–7; and masculinity studies, 23–24; and mythopoetic men's movement, 6–7, 11; and sex role/functionalist paradigm, 29; men's movement approach to, 113, 141, 142n. *See also* Mythopoetic ethic
Socialization, 48, 73; dynamics in men's movement, 9; group processes, 49–50; interruption to sanction breaches, 66–68; management of group discussion, 63–66; readings to support group values, 58–60; removal of men from group, 68–72; role of organic intellectuals, 43–44, 46, 48; selection and initiatory socialization of new members, 53–57, 82–83; statements of group values, 57–58; targeted rituals, 61–63
Social sciences: interdisciplinary approaches, 21, 30–35, 39–40. *See also* Cultural sociology; Gender studies; Microsociology
Speaking stick. *See* Talking stick
Spider web organizational structure, 127
Sports, 30–31
Steinem, Gloria, 38–39

# About the Author

Eric Magnuson is Assistant Professor of Sociology at Loyola Marymount University.